FROM THE EDITORS OF

CONSUMERGUIDE

www.consumerguide.com

The Internet Made Easy for Seniors

With Kris Ann Hegle

Publications International, Ltd.

Kris Ann Hegle frequently writes about the Internet, computers, and new technology. Her work has appeared in magazines for seniors including *Modern Maturity, Prime Times, The Retired Officer Magazine,* and *Arthritis Today.*

Louis Weber, CEO
Publications International, Ltd.
7373 North Cicero Avenue
Lincolnwood, Illinois 60712

Permission is never granted for commercial purposes.

Manufactured in China.

8 7 6 5 4 3 2 1

ISBN: 0-7853-4568-X

Contents

Introduction
Welcome to the Web

A lot of books have been written about the Internet and the World Wide Web, but few of them have focused on the needs and special interests of seniors. Although most seniors haven't grown up "wired," you have been quick to embrace the Internet and use its technology. In fact, mature adults comprise the fastest growing group of new computer and Web users. That's not surprising if you stop to consider that seniors, in general, have more time, money, and interest in world events than their younger counterparts.

Taking time to learn a few Internet basics will change your life. You can use this medium to renew old friendships, send mail to bridge the distance with loved ones, and access information on any subject that interests you.

This book is designed to help make your Internet experience as pleasurable as possible. You can use it as a quick reference guide or as an in-depth tutorial.

Not many people read computer books from cover to cover. Still, take a few minutes to scan the first four chapters, which cover the basics on how the Internet and World Wide Web work. You'll find out why you should go online, learn how to choose an Internet provider, discover tips for navigating the Net, and learn how to find the information you want.

This book also contains several chapters, broken down into categories, of Web sites worth visiting. These sites contain a broad range of information that interests many seniors, and the appendix gives the name, Web address, and short description of some lesser-known sites that contain even *more* useful information.

Throughout the book, key terms appear in bold text. Whenever possible, these terms are defined within the text itself, as well as in the glossary.

Finally, check out the book's CD-ROM, which contains more tutorials, tips, and additional information about many of the exciting Web sites we've reviewed in the book. Designed for ease of use, the CD-ROM is a great way to get your feet wet before you jump in and start "surfing the Web."

* Note that Web sites are changed and redesigned frequently. The information and images provided here are accurate as of press time, but Web sites might have changed since the book and CD-ROM were manufactured.

Chapter 1
Getting on the Information Superhighway

Go to a library, and you can find books about any topic you like: art, science, literature, finance, travel, and more. With the help of a good book and a little imagination, you can go places and experience things you never could otherwise.

Logging on to the Information Superhighway, as the Internet has been dubbed, allows you to do much the same thing. The Internet—or Net—is the world's largest **computer network,** and it contains millions of pages of information about nearly every subject imaginable.

Although most people use the terms **Internet** and **World Wide Web** interchangeably, they are separate entities. The Internet refers to the computers, lines, routers, and other physical equipment that links millions of computers together. When folks talk about "going on the Internet," they're really talking about getting on the World Wide Web. The Web is the graphical, user-friendly portion of the Internet that allows users to send information from one computer to another with ease.

WHAT CAN I DO ON THE WEB?

The Web contains an amazing amount of information that is literally at your fingertips. With a few clicks of the mouse and a couple of keystrokes, you can get the latest news and weather, shop for a new outfit, buy and sell stocks, book a trip to Bora Bora, or send your kids a letter without using a pen, paper, or stamp.

Indeed, **electronic mail** (e-mail) is the most widely used service on the Web. E-mail allows you to send and receive text, graphics, sounds, and videos to and from people all over the world. E-mail also allows you to communicate quickly. Once you've sent an e-mail message, it will be received in a matter of a few hours or even as quickly as a few minutes—regardless of whether it was sent across town or across the world.

Perhaps the best thing the Web offers, though, is a chance to share ideas. People all over the world are talking to each other. They are meeting in **chat**

rooms, which allow users to type and send messages that are received instantly by other users located anywhere in the world. Others are using **instant communication programs,** such as America Online's Instant Messenger, which allow you to send a message that pops up on the recipient's screen while you "talk" to him or her in real time. This is opposed to e-mail, in which a delay is experienced when sending and receiving messages.

Thousands of people have gone one step further and established their own Web sites so they can share their thoughts, ideas, opinions, and outlook for the future. Of course, there's a lot of useless information out there, but there's also a lot of fascinating stuff.

The Internet has changed the way we get information as well. It allows us to gather information very quickly. During the past decade, people have started using the Web as a research tool. Libraries, colleges, universities, and government agencies all have Web sites that are used to disseminate information to the public. Information that once was difficult to find can now be accessed easily, and much of this information is free.

For many people, the Web has also become a form of entertainment. Users can log on to the Web to play games, meet people, or just to see what is going on in the rest of the world.

Electronic commerce (e-commerce) on the Net is changing the way we do business. Auction sites, such as eBay, have become tremendously popular, in large part because they empower consumers. Traditionally, the price of an item is set by the seller. Thanks to the Internet, however, consumers are comparison shopping like never before. Now, instead of paying the seller's price, buyers are engaging in real-time pricing where every price is negotiable or subject to change.

How Can I Get on the Internet?

If you're curious about all the hubbub being made about the Internet, maybe it's time to get online and check it out for yourself. To get on the Net, you'll need to have access to a computer or a set-top box, such as WebTV, which contains a **modem.** A modem, which is short for modulator-demodulator, is the device that lets a computer or set-top box "talk" to another computer through a standard phone line.

If you don't already own a computer or set-top box, you shouldn't feel behind the times. People aged 50 and older currently make up the fastest growing group of new Internet users, and many of these folks are buying a computer or set-top box for the first time.

It's easy to get bogged down in technical aspects when selecting a way to access the Internet. Instead of trying to figure out how much memory your computer should have and what kind of modem is best, start by asking yourself one important question: How do you plan to use a home computer?

Do you want to play games? Do you want to learn how to design and publish your own greeting cards? Or do you plan to use your system primarily to do research? Then again, maybe your needs are simple, and you'd mainly like a computer so you can access the Internet and send and receive e-mail.

When all is said and done, how you plan on using your system will determine what type of system you use to access the Net. Most people access the Internet in one of two ways: via a personal computer (PC) or via a set-top box, such as WebTV.

Access from a PC. Most folks access the Internet via a Windows-based PC. These PCs make up the lion's share of computer sales. Apple computers use the Macintosh (Mac) operating system. Mac users are a loyal bunch. Although 90 percent of the software programs on store shelves are written for PCs, Mac enthusiasts still swear by the Apple for its ease of use and the superior graphics it provides.

If you're thinking about purchasing your first PC, you couldn't have picked a better time to jump into the market. Prices have dropped significantly in the last year, and it's now possible to purchase a Windows-based or Apple system for less than $1,000. If you're interested in an Apple computer, check out the iMac. The iMac costs less than a regular Macintosh, and it offers **plug-and-play access** to the Internet. The computer system itself—including the processor, monitor, and speakers—comes in one piece, which makes it easy to set up. The machine's case also lights up when turned on, and you can choose a machine in one of your favorite colors.

Computer technology changes rapidly, so you might want to check out the latest issue of a consumer buying guide, such as our Consumer Guide™ series, for a recommendation about which PCs are rated as "Best Buys." Your local senior citizens center or a computer club also may provide you with some guidance or suggestions.

Access from a set-top box. If you don't think you'll play games, word process documents, or perform other common computer functions, and you're thinking about getting a computer just to gain access to the Net, you might want to consider buying a set-top box, such as WebTV. Resembling a cable box, WebTV sits on your television set and pipes the Web right onto your TV screen.

The biggest advantage WebTV and other set-top boxes have over computers is price. While an average computer system costs about $1,000, a WebTV unit costs around $200.

Users can purchase an optional wireless keyboard for around $70. However, if you plan to send e-mail on a regular basis, the "optional" keyboard is a necessity. In addition, WebTV allows users to print what they see on their TV screen, so you'll want to invest in a compatible printer.

MYTHS, MISCONCEPTIONS, AND OTHER WEB LEGENDS

Remember when your mother said that if enough people start saying the same thing, sooner or later everybody will believe it's true? Nowhere is this more apparent than the World Wide Web.

E-mail has revolutionized the way we communicate. Instead of waiting days to receive a letter, you can get a message from someone halfway across the world in a matter of minutes. You can then send that message to all the people you know, and before long, the number of people reading the sender's message has multiplied.

Make no mistake, it's probably wise to be a little bit leery when you first get on the Internet. However, a number of myths, misconceptions, and Web legends are still alive and well, and they're being circulated via e-mail. Here are a few of the more common ones.

Myth: The Internet is owned and operated by some entity.

Fact: Nobody "owns" the Internet. The Internet is public domain, decentralized, and owned by no one. However, you can expect to pay a fee to an **Internet Service Provider,** which is the company through which you'll gain access to the Internet.

Myth: Navigating your way around the Web is difficult. You practically have to be a computer wizard to find anything.

Fact: More and more people with little computer savvy are logging on to the Internet. While these folks may experience some difficulties initially, navigating your way around the Web really isn't that difficult, as evidenced by the growing number of grade-school students getting online.

Myth: It's not safe to shop on the Web.

Fact: Perception is everything, and consumers just don't have a lot of confidence when it comes to shopping on the Web. Reputable companies who do business on the Web use secure computer servers to prevent anyone from obtaining your credit card number.

ORIGINS OF THE INTERNET

The Internet's origins date back to 1969 when the U.S. Department of Defense (DOD) founded the Advanced Research Projects Agency Network (ARPANet). Because a missile attack could disable a centralized computer center, the DOD began to form a decentralized communications network.

Working in conjunction with a number of military contractors and universities, ARPANet began to link computers at various locations using several different communication lines. That way, if one or more lines were disabled, the remainder of the network would be able to reroute messages.

This small, decentralized communication system has since grown into a vast global network. During the early 1980s, these interconnected research networks began using the same protocol so they could send data back and forth, and ARPANet became the backbone—or physical connection—between major sites of the newly formed Internet.

In 1991, the Internet really took off after Tim Berners-Lee, a consultant at a Swiss research laboratory, created a program for physicists to share text and graphical information with each other. The program used a standard code, **hypertext markup language** (HTML), for creating and formatting documents. These documents were called Web pages, and they form what is now called the World Wide Web.

You don't want to give out your credit card number at just any old Web site, however. Stick with companies you trust, and do some homework to make sure you're in a secure environment before you place an order. (See Chapter 6 for a list of some popular and secure shops that can be found on the Web.)

Myth: You can get a computer virus that will "crash" your system just by going online.

Fact: You only can get a computer virus if you **download** or save a file that is infected with a computer virus. It is impossible to get a computer virus just by opening an ordinary e-mail message and reading it. To prevent your computer from "crashing" or failing to operate properly, use a virus-protection program that allows you to scan a computer file before you download it. A software shop can help you choose one.

Myth: The Web is full of nothing but pornography.

Fact: Sex sells, and the people peddling explicit materials have found they can reach customers around the globe by marketing themselves on the World

Wide Web. Yes, you can find pornography on the Web—but you can find a lot of other useful information as well.

Myth: The Web changes so fast that it's impossible to learn how to use it.

Fact: Although the Web is evolving, the basic steps you use to get around

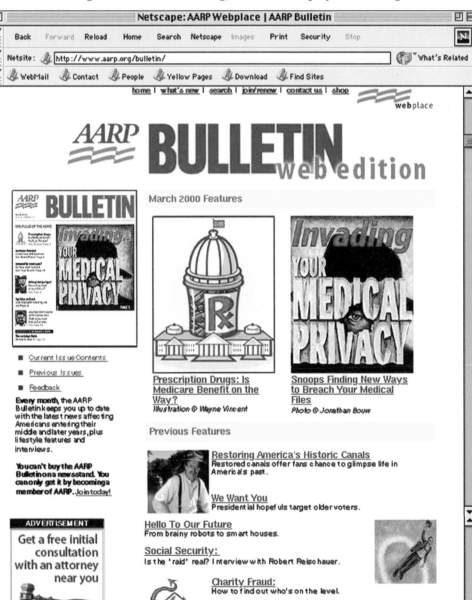

Clicking on a hyperlink will transport you to another Web page. Hyper-linked text is usually under-lined and appears in a color (usually blue) that's different from the regular text found on the page. Icons or graphics also can be hyper-links.

have remained the same and are not that difficult to learn. Once you've learned how to conduct a good online search, send and receive e-mail, and perform other basic functions, the Web really isn't difficult to use.

A MEDIUM FOR THE MASSES

If you're a novice, learning how to use a new computer or set-top box can be a bit intimidating. Remember to be patient with yourself. After all, you didn't grow up playing video games.

Learning how to navigate the Internet is a lot like learning to drive a stick-shift car. At first, you have to think about which gear you should be in and learn how to work the clutch. Before long, however, you're shifting from gear to gear without really thinking about what you're doing.

As you prepare to enter the Information Superhighway, feel free to use this book and the accompanying CD-ROM as your personal driver's manual. In the coming chapters, you'll find directions and instructions on how to get where you want to go. You'll also find eight chapters with Web addresses (which work much like street addresses) for sites you might want to visit along the way.

Chapter 2
Choosing an Internet Provider

The computer or set-top box you've purchased is out of the box and plugged in. You're almost ready to roll. The next thing you need to do is pick an Internet provider, which will charge you a fee to access the Internet. There are two types of Internet providers—**online services** and **Internet Service Providers** (ISPs).

Online services have two parts. The first part gives subscribers access to the World Wide Web. The second part contains "members only" information that can't be found on the Web. All of this information is divided into subject categories, such as travel, finance, and entertainment, that help subscribers find what they're looking for.

Many people who are learning how to navigate their way around the Information Superhighway use an online service. Online services include America Online (AOL), CompuServe, Prodigy, EarthLink, and the Microsoft Network, to name a few.

Online services also provide subscribers with all the software needed to get online and connect to the Internet. This is helpful for people who aren't that familiar with computers. The software provided is easy to install, and most online services provide telephone support if you experience difficulties.

ISPs, on the other hand, only provide a direct connection to the Internet. Subscribers do not receive the organized "members only" categories; they must search and evaluate the information themselves.

While online services are national, ISPs may be national, regional, or local. National ISPs and online services have access numbers in almost every major city in the United States. These allow you to get on the Internet for the price of a local phone call. National ISPs include AT&T WorldNet, Sprint Internet Passport, MCI WorldCom Internet, and others.

Travelers and retirees with two homes usually choose a national ISP or online service for convenience. For example, if you live in Minneapolis, Minnesota, during the summer but spend the winter in Tampa, Florida, you can access a national ISP at either location by dialing a local phone number. However, if you opt to use a local or regional ISP in the Minneapolis area, you'll have to dial long distance to access your ISP account when you're in Florida.

To find out which ISPs are available in your local or regional area, look in your phone book under "Internet Service Providers." Or, log onto the Web at your local library or a friend's computer and check out The List *(www.thelist.com)*, which sorts ISPs by state and area.

When it comes to ISPs and online services, bigger doesn't always mean better. Many local and regional ISPs offer lower prices, superior performance, and better technical support than some national ISPs or online services. Smaller ISPs also are more accessible, particularly if you live in a rural area.

The biggest advantage national ISPs and online services have is **bandwidth**. AT&T WorldNet, Sprint Internet Passport, and MCI WorldCom Internet all have huge, super-fast data networks, or "backbones," that link different regions of the country together and provide users with speedy Internet access.

Both online services and ISPs offer a variety of pricing plans. Some plans charge subscribers by the hour, while others provide unlimited Internet access for a flat monthly fee. In general, however, more time spent online costs you more money.

Regardless of whether you use an online service or an ISP, make sure you're accessing the Internet with a local phone call. If you live in a rural area and don't have local access, see if your Internet provider or phone company has any special pricing plans.

CHOOSING A BROWSER

If you sign up with an online service, such as CompuServe or AOL, you'll use the company's proprietary **browser** to access the Internet. A browser is a software program that allows you to view information on the World Wide Web.

ISPs, on the other hand, may not provide you with a browser. If that's the case, you'll need to choose and install your own browser. The good news is that several browsers are readily available, and most of them can be **downloaded**, or transferred electronically from the company's Web site to your computer's hard drive, for free.

The browser you use will determine how Web pages are displayed on your computer. Different browsers offer different options and tools for navigating the Internet. For example, if you use Microsoft Internet Explorer, the home page for Dr. Weil *(www.drweil.com)* will appear in Microsoft's format. However, if you use Opera as your browser, you can have two Web sites open at the same time, such as Dr. Weil and Dr. Koop *(www.drkoop.com)*, and view them side-by-side.

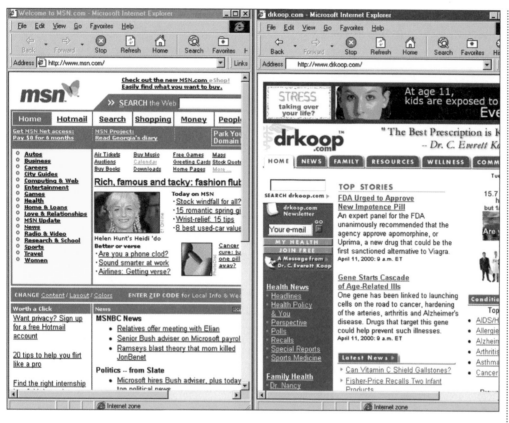

Opera's browser allows users to have two Web sites open at the same time and view them side-by-side. This is handy if you want to compare information about a specific topic.

Although there are many browsers to choose from, the three most popular are Netscape Navigator, Microsoft Internet Explorer, and Opera. Netscape Navigator *(www.netscape.com)* and Microsoft Internet Explorer *(www.microsoft.com)* have many of the same features. These features include good security, a user-friendly format, and the ability to add extra features that will expand the browser's capabilities and enhance your online experience.

If you're using Microsoft Windows as your **operating system**, chances are Microsoft Internet Explorer already has been installed on your computer. The biggest advantage to using this browser is that it's closely integrated with the Microsoft Windows operating system, which provides you with countless options for configuring your system.

Unlike Netscape Navigator and Microsoft Internet Explorer, Opera's browser *(www.opera.com)* isn't free. But for around $35, it may be worth buying if you own an older computer that doesn't have a lot of memory, or space, on its **hard drive**.

Opera won't hog space on your computer's hard drive, and it's packed with features. This browser loads Web pages quickly, allows you to view two Web pages simultaneously, has good security, and gives you the option of magnifying the Web page you're viewing.

THE NEED FOR SPEED

If you've already ventured onto the Web, you know how important it is to get quick access. Web sites are filled with graphics, which take time to transfer or load onto your computer screen.

Like many folks, you already may own a computer and use a modem to access the Internet. Modems transfer information over a regular phone line, and the speed at which they transfer data is measured in **kilobits per second** (Kbps or K). If you have a modem that is slower than 28.8K, consider upgrading to a 56K modem—the fastest currently available.

Unfortunately, the Information Superhighway, like other highways, has a speed limit that's set by the folks at the Federal Communications Commission (FCC). Currently, the FCC allows modems to transfer data at speeds up to 53K.

Still, you'll want to be going as fast as you can when you access the Internet. After all, there's a lot of traffic out there, and you'll want to get where you're going as quickly as possible.

You also may want to consider other Internet connection possibilities, such as a **digital subscriber line** (DSL), an **integrated services digital network** (ISDN) line, or a **cable**, **wireless**, or **satellite** modem. These devices generally offer faster data transmission speeds than a typical modem, but they cost more money.

Before deciding what type of connection is right for you, remember that the kind of equipment you're using to access the Internet may limit your options. For example, if you bought a WebTV unit, you'll be using the unit's internal modem to access the Internet.

Or maybe you own a computer with a modem, but you've decided to pay a little extra each month to connect to the Internet using a super-fast cable connection. If that's the case, you may be limited to using the cable provider that is available in your area, such as Time-Warner Road Runner or AT&T's Cable Network. These services usually determine the Internet browser you'll use.

Some connections may not be available to you. This is particularly true if you live in a rural area. Before you make a decision, consult your local phone book or ask your friendly neighborhood computer buff if he or she knows what Internet connection options are available in your area.

Finally, take a long hard look at what you really need. Cable access is nice, but it's also more expensive. Do you really want to pay $40 to $50 a month for a cable modem if all you plan to do is send and receive e-mail?

Like everything else, technology for accessing the Internet is evolving rapidly. Technology that costs a lot today might be quite affordable in a few years. Hang in there, and periodically reexamine how you're accessing the Internet to make sure you're getting the deal that works best and is most affordable for you.

QUESTIONS TO ASK AN INTERNET PROVIDER

Most Internet providers will ask you to commit to their service for a certain period of time, which might range anywhere from a month to three years. Regardless of whether you choose an online service or ISP to serve as your Internet provider, take a little time to research your options and ask some questions. If you've never signed up with an Internet provider before, here's a list of questions you might want to ask.

- Can I access your service with a local phone call?
- How much do you charge for unlimited monthly service? Do you offer hourly rate plans? How much do you charge if I exceed the hourly rate limit?
- Is there a fee to set up my account?
- Do you provide set-up assistance? Do you provide technical support if I have a problem connecting to the Web? Is it difficult to reach technical support?
- Do you provide all the software, including a Web browser, needed to access the Internet and send and receive e-mail?
- Will I have a problem connecting to your service during peak usage hours?
- Will you provide me with free space on your server for hosting a personal Web page if I decide to develop one?

Ways to Access the Internet		
Method	Pros	Cons
STANDARD MODEM • Speed is less than 56K	• Only additional expense is for an Internet provider, since new computers and set-top boxes come equipped with a modem	• Can't talk on the phone and be on the Internet at the same time (unless you add another phone line to your home) • Doesn't provide two-way continuous Internet access
CABLE • Speed ranges from 400K to 4 megabits per second (Mbps)	• Provides two-way continuous access • Doesn't tie up phone line • Usually provides users with best value for the price	• Not available everywhere • User can't choose own Internet provider • Heavy Internet usage by neighbor may slow down connection because cable lines are shared
ISDN • Provides access speeds up to 128K	• User can receive phone calls while on the Internet • User can choose Internet provider • More consistent speed than cable modem because there's one user per line	• Requires special equipment, and installation is usually expensive • Doesn't provide two-way continuous Internet access • Not available everywhere

Ways to Access the Internet (continued)		
Method	Pros	Cons
DSL • Provides access speeds from 144K to 1.7 Mbps	• Provides two-way continuous access • More consistent speed than cable modem because there's one user per line • Some DSL providers will split an existing phone line so a second phone line isn't required • User can choose Internet provider	• Installation is expensive and time consuming • Not available everywhere
SATELLITE • Downloads as fast as 400K	• Will work anywhere there's a phone line and open sky • Provides continuous access when downloading	• Must use a regular phone line and modem to upload information and send it across the Internet • Technology still under development • Requires special equipment • User can't choose own Internet provider
WIRELESS • Promises access speeds 100 times faster than cable or DSL	• Provides continuous access • Reaches places phone wires and cable networks don't • Cheaper to install than underground wires • User can choose Internet provider	• Technology is still being developed • Bad weather can hinder connections • Requires special equipment

Chapter 3
Navigating the Net

Your machine is set up, and your browser has been installed. It's time to get on the Net. Although you'll log on to the Internet—the lines, routers, and network of computers that form this medium—you'll actually be spending most of your time on the World Wide Web. The Web, if you remember, is the user-friendly portion of the Internet that contains text, sound, and graphics.

Although there are many different types of Web browsers, every Web page shares some common features. That's because Web pages are created using **hypertext markup language** (HTML). HTML is the standard code used for creating and formatting Web pages. Unlike many other software programs, it allows people to view pages on the Web regardless of the computer or operating system they use.

The screen on page 21 shows what a typical Web page looks like in Netscape. (Note that your screen might look a bit different if you use a different browser.) Across the top of the page, you'll see a **toolbar** (#1) that contains **icons**, or tiny pictures. Icons give visual clues about a browser's capabilities.

Starting from the left side of the toolbar, you will notice two buttons with arrows. The **Forward** button allows you to jump forward in a document; the **Back** button lets you go back to view the last screen you viewed. There's also a **Reload** button that reloads the Web page if you click on the button.

After surfing around a bit, you may decide it's time to return to the site's main page. This page is called the **home page**. To get to the home page, click on the icon labeled **Home**.

The next icon, **Search**, allows you to conduct searches for anything on the Web. A drop-down menu along the top of your screen (not shown) offers a **Bookmark** option, in which you can store the locations of your favorite Web sites. There's even a menu item called **Go**, which will display a list of Web sites you've visited recently.

Just below the toolbar, you'll find the **Universal Resource Locator** (URL) (#2). URLs are the "street addresses" of sites on the Information Superhighway. Like a street address, no two URLs are alike.

All URLs follow a standard addressing system, which primarily uses lower-case letters. For example, ***http://www.whitehouse.gov*** is the URL or Web

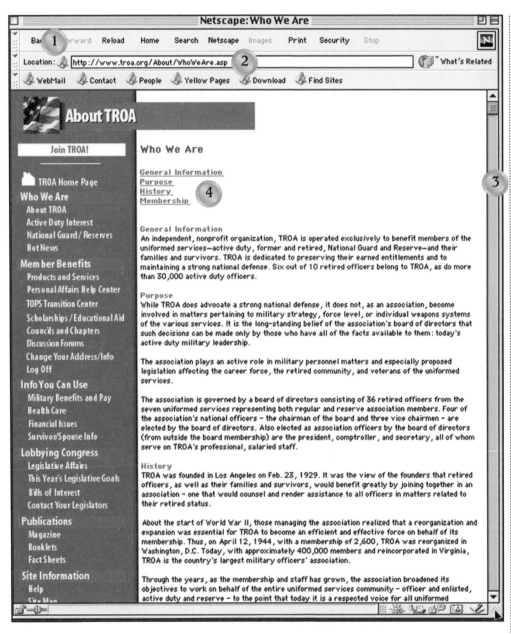

address for the White House. All URLs begin with "http," which stands for **hypertext transfer protocol**, the standard document interface used on the Web. The letters "www" tell you that you are accessing the document from the part of the Internet known as the World Wide Web.

Next comes the name of the company or organization you are trying to contact, which in this case is the White House. The last three letters of a URL are called the **domain name**. The domain name indicates the type of organization you're trying to contact. The domain name ".gov" indicates you are trying to reach a government site.

Domain names include:

.gov—government sites

.com—companies or commercial businesses

.edu—educational sites

.net—network sites

.org—private or nonprofit organizations

.mil—U.S. military sites

Understanding Web addresses can be very helpful. For instance, let's say you didn't know the Web address for the Department of Veterans Affairs. Well, you can probably guess it. You know the address will begin with "http://www." Because the government is the mother of all acronym makers, odds are the Veteran's Administration uses the acronym VA in its Web address. Because the VA is a government agency, the domain name is ".gov." When you put it all together, *presto*, you have the address you need: ***http://www.va.gov***.

If you find a particular Web page that is worth visiting again, you may want to "bookmark" it. To bookmark a site, click on **Bookmarks** in Netscape Navigator, **Favorites** in Microsoft Internet Explorer, or **Hot list** in Opera. This will allow you to save the URL so you don't have to retype it every time you want to visit the site. Just choose it from your list, and you're there!

On the right side of your screen, you'll find a **scroll bar** (#3). The scroll bar allows you to move up and down within a Web document.

As you move through Web documents, you'll notice that certain words appear in colors that are different from the surrounding text. These words are **hyperlinks** (#4). A hyperlink may be a word, a group of words, an icon, or an image that, when you click on it, will take you to a different document or another part of the same document.

Notice how the cursor turns into a hand when it moves over a hyperlink.

Use your mouse to move the I-beam cursor over a hyperlink. Notice the I-beam cursor changes into the shape of a hand when it passes over a hyperlink. Just beneath the hand, you'll sometimes see (depending on your system) a tiny dialog box. This dialog box contains a brief description of the information you'll find if you click on this hyperlink. Often, the URL of the Web site that the hyperlink will take you to appears along the bottom of your screen as well.

WHAT IS E-MAIL?

Now that you know some Web-page basics, it's time to get down to business. If you're like most folks, you signed up with an Internet provider primarily so you could send and receive e-mail.

When you sign up with an Internet provider, you'll be asked to choose an e-mail address. An e-mail address is a unique code that lets you receive messages, just as your street address lets you receive letters from the post office.

E-mail addresses consist of four parts: a user name, which can be your name or a fictional nickname; the @ (at) sign; the name of the organization where your e-mail account resides; and a three-letter code (the domain name) that indicates the nature of the organization.

For example, John Doe's e-mail address is johndoe@ compuserve.com. The user name is johndoe; CompuServe is the name of the Internet provider he uses; and .com identifies that CompuServe is a company or commercial business.

The best part about e-mail is that it's fast. Once you've sent an e-mail, it will be received in a matter of a few minutes—regardless of whether it was sent across town or across the world. That's why many Internet users refer to the U.S. Postal Service as "snail mail."

Like regular mail, however, e-mail has its problems. If the recipient doesn't have continuous Internet access, his or her Internet provider must store your message. When the recipient logs on the Internet, the Internet provider will forward your message.

FREE E-MAIL SERVICES

In addition to the regular e-mail account you get from your Internet provider, you may want to set up a free e-mail account. There are several reasons why you should consider setting up a free e-mail account.

First, if you use a free Web-based e-mail service, such as Yahoo! *(www.yahoo.com)* or HotMail *(www.hotmail.com)*, you don't even need to own a computer. All you need is access to a computer with an Internet connection and a browser.

The second advantage is you can make your free e-mail account as temporary or permanent as you want. Setting up a free e-mail account will give you another user ID, which you can use in chat rooms and other public places.

Setting up a free e-mail account has another advantage: Because you have an e-mail account that is independent of your Internet provider, your e-mail address won't change if you change your Internet provider.

If the recipient's computer system is temporarily down, he or she may not be able to get your message or send a reply. E-mail can get lost, for example, if you mistype the recipient's address; your message could end up in the wrong mailbox.

It's easy to mistype an e-mail address. Remember that e-mail addresses never contain any spaces. Sometimes an underline or hyphen is used where a space might typically be, such as between a person's first and last names. For example, John Doe's e-mail address could be john_doe@aol.com but could not be john doe@aol.com.

SENDING MESSAGES

Because it's all too easy to goof up an e-mail address, consider taking time to set up an **address book**. If you're like most folks, many of the e-mail messages you send will go to the same people. By creating an address book, you can avoid typing the same person's e-mail address over and over again. Setting up an address book also allows you to send the same message to several different people without doing a lot of work.

To send an e-mail message using Microsoft Internet Explorer, click on the **Mail** icon in your browser's toolbar. A pop-up menu will appear. Choose New Message to compose a new e-mail.

*This is what a typical e-mail box looks like in a free e-mail program. Notice the **Addresses** button that allows you to store commonly used e-mail addresses.*

| INBOX | COMPOSE | SEND | SAVE DRAFT | CANCEL |

From:
To: _____ Address Book
Subject: _____
Cc: _____ Bcc: _____
Signature [No Signature ⬍] Save: ☐ outgoing message to sent folder

[Attachments] [Spell Check]

COMPOSE
FOLDERS
OPTIONS
HELP
ADDRESSES
LOGOUT

SEND SAVE DRAFT CANCEL

The screen where you will compose your message will appear. You'll notice this screen has several fields. Fill in the **To** line with the recipient's e-mail address. If you believe you will be sending this person e-mail in the future, add the person's name to your electronic address book. The next time you send that person an e-mail, you can open your address book by clicking on the word **To**. Select the recipient's name, click on it, and their address will automatically appear in the **To** line of your message.

Next fill in the **Subject** line, and then type your message. When you're done, click **Send**. When you send the message, your computer will automatically put your e-mail address in the **From** line.

Another timesaving feature of e-mail is that it allows you to reply to a message without having to set up a completely new e-mail. To reply, simply click on the **Reply** button, type your message, and click **Send**. By doing this, you'll avoid retyping the recipient's address and filling in the subject line.

YOU'VE GOT JUNK MAIL

You don't know why the LuvDr@aol.com has sent you an e-mail, but he has. Apparently he knows you—or at least knows your e-mail address. You open his e-mail only to find a message urging you to visit a pornographic Web site.

You're mad and a little disgusted. Why did you get this type of e-mail? Chances are, the LuvDr bought your e-mail address from a list broker. Then again, maybe he was lurking in one of the chat rooms you visited last week.

You can expect to receive a fair amount of junk e-mail, or **spam**, if you go online. Spam is the latest form of direct marketing. Like junk mail that fills your home's mailbox, spam clogs computer networks and slows the delivery of important e-mail.

Online services and ISPs have spent millions of dollars trying to stop spam. They've bought new servers to handle the increased flow of mail, installed filtering software to block the mail entirely, and paid legal fees to prosecute some of the worst offenders. Still, spammers continue to find ways to get around the system.

You'll never be able to eliminate spam entirely. However, there are a few preventive measures you can take to keep spam from clogging your online mailbox.

First, review each Web site's privacy policy before giving out your e-mail address or other personal information. If no privacy policy can be found, consider taking your business elsewhere.

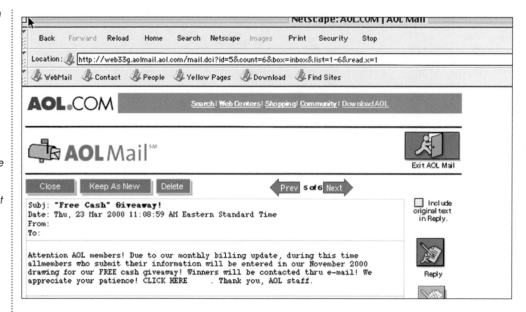

Beware of spam e-mail, particularly if you belong to an online service. Con artists, impersonating employees from the service, have been known to send e-mails that try to entice subscribers to divulge their user passwords or credit card information.

If you plan on visiting chat rooms or other places frequented by spammers, set up an additional user ID or screen name. You can do this by setting up a free e-mail account. (See Free E-mail Services on page 23 for more details on how to do this.)

If you subscribe to an online service, such as AOL, create another screen name. Online services allow subscribers to use several screen names, and you should have a dedicated screen name you use in public environments such as chat rooms.

Creating another user ID or screen name may seem a little silly, but it's a good way to avoid getting spammed. It's also a great way to ensure your anonymity, particularly if you use an online service and have created a user profile that contains some personal information.

Finally, never respond to spam—even if it's to request that your name be removed from the spammer's mailing list. Many people unwittingly confirm their e-mail address by replying to spam.

COMPUTER VIRUSES AND E-MAIL

Receiving unsolicited e-mail isn't just annoying—it can be dangerous. Some of the spam you receive may contain an **attachment** file. However, unlike a

regular e-mail message, you must download or transfer an attachment to your computer's hard drive before you can open and view it.

An attachment may contain a **computer virus**, which is a software program designed to destroy data stored on your system or cause an undesired action to be performed by your computer. For example, downloading and opening an attachment could launch a "sniffer," or Trojan horse program, that steals and spreads your passwords to others.

Although you should be leery about downloading an e-mail attachment, it's OK to open and read an e-mail message. Contrary to what you may have heard, you can't "catch" a computer virus just by opening and reading an ordinary e-mail.

It's also possible to catch a computer virus by downloading infected software from the Web. Offline, your computer can catch a virus by inserting an infected floppy disk or CD-ROM in your computer.

Several good **anti-virus programs** are on the market, and you should use one of them. When it comes to viruses and your computer, it's best to play it safe. Before downloading software from the Internet, opening an e-mail attachment, or using a floppy disk or CD-ROM given to you by a friend, use an anti-virus program to scan for viruses.

E-MAIL IS NOT PRIVATE

If you don't want your message to be viewed by a third party, don't send it by e-mail. E-mail messages aren't secure. Anybody who has access to the recipient's computer can open your message and read it.

For example, if you plan to shop online, never put personal information, such as your credit card number or Social Security number, in an e-mail message. Someone could use this information for fraudulent purposes. (There are safe ways to shop with credit cards online. These are discussed on page 31.)

Furthermore, e-mail messages can be forwarded easily to other people. If you feel like sounding off, don't do it by e-mail. You never know who might wind up reading what you've written.

If you subscribe to an online service, watch out for scam artists impersonating company employees. These scam artists use a variety of ploys, such as offering one month of free Internet service, to get members to disclose their credit card information, password, or other personal information. Should someone contact you to "verify" this type of information, contact your online service or ISP immediately to report the attempted fraud.

OTHER WAYS TO COMMUNICATE

E-mail is just one form of online communication. You can also find chat rooms on the Web in which people "talk" to each other by typing messages.

If you use an online service or national ISP, you might have access to an **Internet relay chat** (IRC). IRCs (also called instant messaging programs) allow you to talk one-on-one with a friend in **real time**.

Although it's fun to meet people online, think twice before revealing any personal information about yourself—even if you chat with a particular person on a regular basis. People might not be who they say they are. They may lie about their sex, age, or where they live because you have no way of verifying any of this information.

When it comes to communicating on the Web, don't be afraid to get out there and mingle a little. But use your street smarts.

Another good place to meet people online is through a **newsgroup**. The Web contains thousand of newsgroups, which are ongoing discussions about a particular topic, such as sports, TV shows, or politics. Newsgroups contain a database of messages. You can post a question, or you can respond to someone else's question or message. If you're interested in taking part in a newsgroup, check out Deja.com *(www.deja.com)*.

Chat rooms are great places to meet people. This chat room in Yahoo! allows you to send an instant message to another chatter.

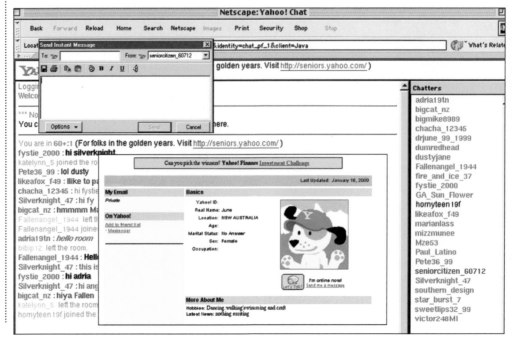

Mailing lists, like newsgroups, are made up of participants who discuss certain topics by e-mail. To participate, you must subscribe to a list so all new postings will be e-mailed to you.

Keep in mind you might receive dozens of e-mail messages each day if you're on a mailing list. However, it's just as easy to unsubscribe to a mailing list as it is to subscribe to one.

Take Time to Learn Some "Netiquette"

You're sitting at home in front of your computer, you're wearing your fuzzy slippers, and you're typing away to a new friend you've met in a chat room. In this kind of relaxed setting, it's easy to forget that what you type may be misinterpreted.

Remember that visual clues and voice intonation can't be conveyed over the Web. When sending messages across the Web, keep the following Netiquette tips in mind:

- Don't write e-mail messages using all capital letters. The recipient will feel like YOU ARE SHOUTING. Instead, enclose the text you want to emphasize in asterisks.

- Always fill in the **Subject** line of an e-mail message. This lets a recipient know why you are writing.

- Spell check your messages before you send them. You will be judged by the quality of your writing.

- Never forward chain e-mail.

- When you're online, adhere to the same standards of conduct you observe in everyday life.

- Forgive others' mistakes. When someone makes a mistake—whether it's a spelling error or a seemingly stupid question—be kind about it. People who point out Netiquette violations often sound ruder than those who violate them.

Staying Safe Online

The Web contains the biggest shopping mall in the world. Web stores are always open, there aren't any crowds, and there are no pushy salesclerks.

Most online shopping is done by credit card. If you use your credit card online, make sure you do so in a secure environment.

There are a couple of different ways to tell if you're on a secure Web page. The Web address, or URL, is slightly different on a secured Web page. Most URLs begin with "http," which stands for hypertext transfer protocol—the set of standards that allows Web users to exchange information. However, if you're on a secure Web page the URL will begin with "https."

The "s" in "https" stands for **Secure Sockets Layer** (SSL). Most online merchants use SSL technology to encrypt (or scramble) your credit card informa-

tion while it's being transmitted over the Internet. SSL, which is the industry's standard security protocol, makes it extremely difficult for anyone to decode your credit card information.

However, not all sites use SSL to secure transactions. Check your browser to see if you're secure. In Netscape Navigator and Microsoft Internet Explorer, a locked

padlock icon will appear in the bottom left corner of your screen when you're on a secure Web page. If the Web page is unsecure, the padlock will be open.

Before leaving a cybershop, jot down the business's address and phone number. You might need this information later if something goes wrong with your order.

TIPS FOR SAFE SHOPPING

It's 2 A.M. and you're heading out to the mall—the online mall, that is. Unlike your neighborhood mall, Web shops are open 24 hours a day, 7 days a week.

If you're concerned about giving out your credit card number over the Internet, you have a legitimate fear. Electronic commerce has grown tremendously in the past few years and so has the number of con artists who do business on the Web.

Before you plunk down your plastic and say, "Hasta la VISA" to your money, take a little time to make sure your transaction is taking place in a secure environment. Here are a few handy tips you should follow when shopping online.

- Put it on your plastic. The Fair Credit Billing Act gives you certain rights, which include the right to challenge charges and withhold payment if you think you've been swindled. Nearly all credit card companies will protect you for any misuse over $50. Using a credit card will also provide you with proof that the transaction occurred.

- Be sure to be secure. Make sure you're placing your order in a secure environment. Secure Web pages begin with "https." Also, your browser will display a locked padlock or key in a lower corner of your screen if you're on a secure Web page.

- When in doubt, get out. Don't be impressed by a glitzy Web page or believe a merchant's claim that its Web site is secure. If you can't determine whether a particular Web site is secure, take your business elsewhere.

- Print a receipt. After placing your order, write down or print the dollar amount you've spent. It's also a good idea to print out information about how you can contact the merchant if there's a problem.

Chapter 4
Seek and You Shall Find

Searching for information on the Web has been compared to looking for a needle in a haystack. The Web contains millions of pages of information, and much of this information is unorganized. Finding the information you want on the Web can seem a little daunting at first, but it's not impossible. In order to conduct a good search, you'll need to know a few basics.

You'll be using one of two kinds of tools to search the Web. The first tool is a **Web directory**. A Web directory organizes information into broad categories that progressively get more specific. The second tool is called a **search engine**. Search engines examine Web documents by **keyword**. Keywords are terms that correspond to or describe the things you're searching for.

Now, here's where things can start to get confusing. Each directory and search engine has its own set of rules. Currently, there's no standardization among the various directories and search engines found on the Web. Because of this, a keyword or phrase that works well with one search engine might produce totally different results with another.

So how do people find what they're looking for? Experienced searchers use more than one search tool. If you're a new Web user, however, remembering different sets of rules for different search tools can get a little confusing.

Many novices never take time to learn the rules for even *one* search tool. These folks inevitably wind up jumping from hyperlink to hyperlink without ever finding the information they're seeking. This activity is called **surfing**. Surfing can be fun, but it can also waste precious time if you need to find something in a hurry.

If you're just starting out, find a search tool you like, and take time to learn some of its advanced features. Once you've mastered it, learning how to use another search tool will be much simpler.

The following describes some of the Web's more popular search tools. To aid readers, a box of "Fast Facts" summarizing the major features of each search tool is included in each section.

YAHOO! WE'RE ON THE WEB
The Yahoo! *(www.yahoo.com)* home page sorts information into topics and

subtopics. These topics and subtopics form a directory, which can be used to search the Web.

Using a directory allows you to move from a general to a specific topic. By following the links in each subject category, you can "drill down" and find the information you need.

Let's say you are looking for information about high blood pressure. This information would be in the **Health** category. Beneath this heading is a hyper-link for **Diseases**. Click on **Diseases**, and several subtopics will appear.

Here, you will see a link for **Heart Disease**. Click on that, and more subtopics will appear. Select **Hypertension@** from this list, and click on it. A list of perti-nent Web sites will appear, including a hyperlink for information on high blood pressure from the American Heart Association.

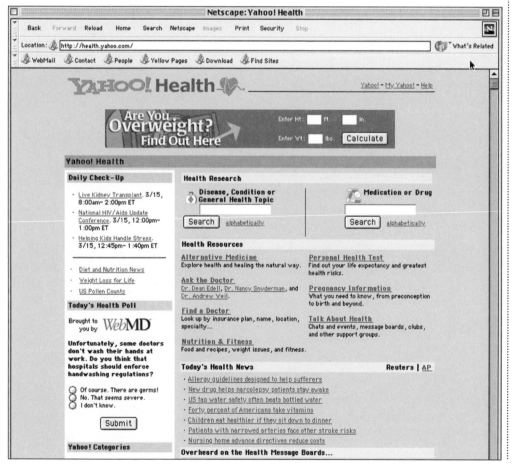

Notice what happens if you begin a key-word search while in the **Health** *cate-gory. Yahoo! will give you the option to search for a* **Disease, Condition or General Health Topic,** *or a* **Medication or Drug**.

In addition to allowing users to browse for information by subject, Yahoo! also lets visitors search by keyword. To conduct a keyword search, type the words "high blood pressure" in the query box on the Yahoo! home page. Be sure to put quotes at the beginning and end of this phrase. Now, click the Search button.

A page of results will appear on your screen. At the top, you will see that Yahoo! found 0 categories and 12 sites for "high blood pressure." The second site listed on the results page contains information on high blood pressure from the American Heart Association. In this case, doing a keyword search yielded results much faster than drilling down for the same information using the Yahoo! directory.

Notice what happens, however, if you go back to the Yahoo! home page and enter the words **high blood pressure** in the query box without surrounding the phrase in quotation marks. This time, the results page found 1 category and 13 sites for high blood pressure. By excluding the quotes, you get slightly different results. Like many search tools, Yahoo! uses **Boolean logic** to search the Web. Boolean logic allows you to refine your search by arranging keywords in a meaningful order and then searching for them as a phrase, rather than as individual words. To do this in Yahoo!, put your keywords inside quotes. (For more information about how Boolean logic works, see the section titled Hints for Better Hits on page 45.)

Now let's try combining a directory search with a keyword search. To do this, you'll need to go back to the Yahoo! home page. Since you know the information you're seeking on high blood pressure is health-related, click on **Health**. You'll be transported to a search-results page that has a query box at the top. Notice the query box on this page looks a little different.

Next to the **Search** button is a pull-down menu that, when you click on it, gives you the option to search **all of Yahoo!** or **just this category**.

Select **just this category** and type the words "high blood pressure" in the adjacent query box. Make sure to put this phrase in quotes. Click **Search** and a new results page will appear.

This search method gives you 0 categories and 10 sites for "high blood pressure." Now try the same search without using quotes. Yahoo! now finds 1 category and 11 sites for high blood pressure.

FAST FACTS ABOUT YAHOO!

- Good tool if you want to search by category
- Allows users to search by keyword as well
- Uses "AND," "OR," and other Boolean logic symbols
- Searches for words in quotes as phrases
- Allows users to search by title and URL

You've just seen for yourself how using different search methods can yield different results—even when you use the same search tool. Just as there are several different routes you could use to drive to your friend's house, there are several different routes you can use on the Information Superhighway to reach the information destination you're seeking.

Another interesting feature of Yahoo! is that it allows you to search a document by title or URL, which is a Web site's address. Place a **t:** in front of a keyword if you want to find a Web page that contains your keyword in its title. Place a **u:** in front of a keyword to find a URL that contains that particular word.

Before leaving Yahoo!, take another look at the home page. You'll notice that Yahoo! offers free e-mail service, and it provides links to shopping, news, sports, travel, and other resources. Because Yahoo! contains resources to other databases found on the Web, it is referred to as a **Web portal**.

Sound confusing? It is a little bit. The difference between directories, search engines, and Web portals is blurring. Tools used to search the Web have evolved to provide users with more search options and services than ever before. For now, don't worry about trying to distinguish between a directory, a search engine, or a Web portal. Instead, concentrate on mastering some basic search skills.

PURSUE IT ON THE WEB WITH LYCOS

Lycos *(www.lycos.com)* bills itself as "Your Personal Internet Guide." Lycos derives its name from the Latin word *Lycosidae*, a type of wolf spider that catches its prey by pursuing it.

Although Lycos began as a search engine, this site has evolved so you can search by either category or keyword. Lycos also is a Web portal, and it offers many services, such as chat room access, free e-mail, travel guides, and more.

Make no mistake, there's a lot going on at Lycos. The big question for visitors, however, is how to take advantage of it all.

Let's begin by conducting a search. Enter the words "discount travel" in the query box. Since you're searching for that phrase, be sure to put it in quotes. Now click on **Go Get It**. A page of search results will appear.

FAST FACTS ABOUT LYCOS

- Good tool for keyword searches
- Allows users to search by category as well
- Uses "AND," "OR," and other Boolean logic symbols
- Searches for phrases in quotes
- Allows users to search by title or URL

Lycos is a Web portal as well as a search engine. Visitors can find many links to other Web-based data-bases and services here, such as chat rooms, e-mail, and travel guides.

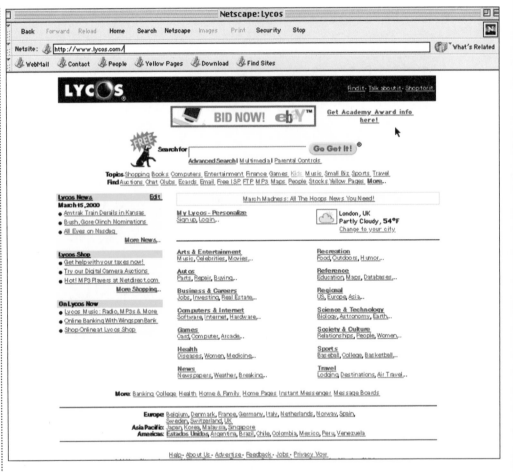

Notice Lycos will allow you to continue sorting this information. You can choose to sort by **Categories**, **Web Sites**, **News & Media**, and **Web Pages**. Clicking on each one of these options will yield a different list of search results.

For example, if you want to find Web sites that talk about discount travel, you should click on **Web Sites**. However, if you want to see a list of articles that have been written about this subject, you should click on **News & Media**.

Lycos' **Advanced Search** link really helps users fine-tune their queries. You can choose how Lycos searches for the word or phrase you're seeking, pick the number of search results you want displayed on a page, and tell the search engine to look for the phrase by document, title, or URL. The **Advanced Search** page also contains several other categories, such as **Navigating Lycos**, **Tools**,

Build, **Find**, and **Buy**, which contain additional links to help you find the information you're seeking.

EXCITE—WHAT A CONCEPT!

In Yahoo! and Lycos you searched by topic and by keyword or phrase. In Excite *(www.excite.com)* you will search by concept.

Searching by concept is really helpful, particularly if you can't think of a good keyword to describe what you're looking for. Excite contains an Intelligent Search tool that looks for concepts that are similar to the words you've entered

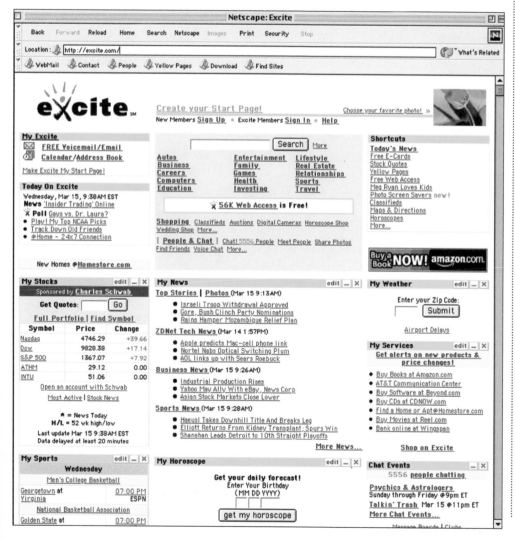

Excite allows you to search by keyword. To narrow your search, click one of the hyperlinked divisions below the search box.

FAST FACTS ABOUT EXCITE

- Searches by concept
- Does not use quotes when searching by concept
- Allows searches by keyword or phrase when using the **Advanced Search** option
- Ranks results by relevance and gives you the option to **Search for more documents like this one**

and provides links to relevant information. Once you've sent your search query, Excite will display the results, which are ranked by relevance, and give you the option to **Search for more documents like this one**.

For example, let's say you collect rare coins and you want to find a Web site where you can bid on some nifty old coins. To find what you're seeking, enter the phrase "bid on rare coins" in the query box on Excite's home page. Then click **Search**.

A results page will appear that lists several places where you can bid on or buy rare coins online. Notice the results are ranked by relevance. It would appear that Coin Universe and Heritage Rare Coin Galleries are good places to begin your search.

Before linking to these sites, however, you can choose to look at other possible matches by clicking on **Search for more documents like this one**. Or go to the top of the results page. Just beneath the query box is a list of words you can add to your query to make it even more specific.

If you'd rather search by keyword or phrase, Excite's **Advanced Search** feature can accommodate you. To view the advanced search options, click on **More**, which is located just to the right of the search box on Excite's home page.

ALTAVISTA—THE VIEW FROM ABOVE

AltaVista (*altavista.digital.com*) is a favorite among intermediate to experienced Web users because it allows them to fashion a highly detailed query. That's because AltaVista uses **full-text indexing**, which means that every word on a Web page is put into a database.

FAST FACTS ABOUT ALTAVISTA

- Allows users to conduct a very detailed query
- Great tool for finding the Web address of a company, business, organization, or government agency
- Contains a database you can search for images, audio, and video files
- Has the ability to translate sites created in English into several other languages

AltaVista allows you to translate or search for sites in many languages. Click on the box titled **any language***, and a drop-down box appears. Highlight the language you desire.*

Netscape: AltaVista - Search

Back Forward Reload Home Search Netscape Images Print Security Stop

Location: http://www.altavista.com/ What's Related

WebMail Contact People Yellow Pages Download Find Sites

alta**vista**: SEARCH

smart is beautiful

Search Live! Shopping Raging Bull Free Internet Access Email

HealthCentral Rx Over 23000 Products

Deals of the Day amazon.com.

Need a DVD Shop here now!

Search Advanced Search Images MP3/Audio Video Try our NEW Search Centers

Find this: _____ [Search] [any language ▼]

Example: +weather+forecast

Find Results on: ○ The Web ○ News ○ Discussion Groups ○ Products

Help
Family Filter off
Language Settings

My Live! Money Sports Women **Health** Travel Real Estate News Jobs Translate Entertainment Chats

Tax Center *New!* Message Boards Free Internet Access Email Yellow Pages People Finder Directions Home Pages

Breaking News

- 30 Hurt in Amtrak Derailment
- Apple Predicts Cell Phone Link
- Bob Knight Accused of Choking
- First Net Insider Trading Case
- Spielberg Helms Kubrick Film

Stock Quotes Symbol Lookup

[Get Quote(s)]

What's On AltaVista Now

Hurry!: $1M bracket game ends tomorrow

March Madness: Regions, scores, message boards

Print It: Oscars ballot
King Book: Online horror
Health: College drinking
Home: Rent or buy?
Zoo: Animal cams

Free download: AltaVista Alert

Fast Find:
Yellow Pgs | Directions | Translation | TV

Raging Topics on the Boards

Web Directory

Arts & Entertainment
Movies, TV, Music...

Autos
Classic, Dealers, Manufacturers...

Business & Finance
Industries, Jobs, Investing...

Computers
Software, Hardware, Graphics...

Games
Video, Role-Playing, Gambling...

Health & Fitness
Conditions, Medicine, Alternative...

Home & Family
Kids, Houses, Consumers...

Internet
Chat, Email, WWW...

News & Media
Online, Magazines, Newspapers...

Recreation & Travel
Food, Outdoors, Humor...

Reference
Maps, Education, Libraries...

Regional
US, Canada, UK, Europe...

Science
Biology, Psychology, Physics...

Shopping
Auction, Compare, WWW Sites...

Society & Culture
People, Religion, Issues...

Sports
Baseball, Soccer, Football...

World
Deutsch, Español, Svenska...

Go Shopping Now!

Handheld User Reviews *New!*
Palm has buzz, but other devices have fans, too. more...

Find Hot Deals
- Free Virex 5.8!
- Nintendo64 Games >$40!

Popular Searches
- Barbie
- Sony

Compare Prices
- Pioneer DVD/CD Player
- Epson Photo PC

Featured Sponsors

- Say, "I adore you" in jewelry – Miadora
- Find a new job with AltaVista Careers!
- Click Here to Shop online at AltaVista!
- Click to Personalize with AV Live

Välkommen i AltaVista!

Hot Searches

AltaVista Search Guides
Use the power of the Web to find what you are looking for:

Find a Pet Get a New Job

This is more comprehensive than **keyword-text indexing**, which puts words and phrases in a database based on their location and frequency. If a word or phrase is only mentioned once or twice on a Web page, that site might not be included in a keyword text index.

So how does AltaVista determine good matches? By checking to see whether all or some of the words in your query appear within a particular Web site. Sites that match all of your query words will appear toward the top of your results page.

AltaVista also counts how many times the search engine finds a query word in a Web site and then looks to see where the query word appears. For example, if one of your keywords appears in the Web site's title or within the first few paragraphs of text, the match gets a better score.

If you're looking for a company, business, or government agency's Web site, AltaVista is the search engine to use. AltaVista uses a technology called Real-Names that checks your query against an internal database of names and slogans. If a match is found, you'll be pointed to the organization's home page.

If you're the creative type, you'll appreciate AltaVista's searchable database of more than 25 million images, audio, and video files. AltaVista also will translate Web pages created in English into other languages, such as French, German, Italian, Spanish, and Portuguese. To do this, click on **Translate** underneath the document you would like to view on the results page.

Like many other search engines, AltaVista uses Boolean logic. You also can use a **wildcard** when searching. A wildcard is denoted by an * symbol. For example, the query **boat*** on AltaVista will return information on boats, boaters, boating, etc.

FAST FACTS ABOUT GOOGLE

- Great tool for simple searches
- Searches for every word in a query
- Doesn't recognize the Boolean operator "OR"
- Allows you to jump directly to the first Web page that matches your query

GOOGLE AND ALL THAT GOBBLEDYGOOK

If you're tired of Web portals that seem to have links to everything but the kitchen sink, you will appreciate Google's *(www.google.com)* simplicity. This no-nonsense site is the place to go if you want to conduct a simple search.

What's nice about Google is that it's straightforward. Type a few words in the query box, and click on **Google Search**. Google performs "AND" queries by default, so it will only return pages that include all of the search terms entered. Consequently, Google doesn't recognize "OR," because "OR" searches for either word in your query.

Did you get too many hits? That's not a big deal if you're using Google, because Google only returns Web pages that contain all the words in your query. To narrow a search, all you need to do is add more words to your original query.

When searching the Web, Google examines the words on a Web site and ranks them based on their location, font size, and other factors. Google then uses a technology called PageRank to decide which documents you would like to see first.

Google has a knack for returning great results for simple searches. To go directly to the first Web site that Google matches for your query, click on **I'm Feeling Lucky**.

The basic premise behind PageRank is that good Web pages contain links to other good Web pages. In fact, Google is so confident that you'll like the way PageRank organizes results that you can click on **I'm Feeling Lucky** and get sent directly to the first Web page it finds for your query.

Google also allows users to search by phrase using quotation marks. Words enclosed within quotes will appear together in the search results.

If you need a search tool that can handle a complex query, you should go elsewhere. For most searches, Google provides fast and efficient results.

HotBot and the Land of Neon Colors

If you can handle the neon green that jumps out and greets you at HotBot *(www.hotbot.com)*, you've got it made. HotBot challenges users to "Search Smarter," and it gives them a number of tools to do so.

HotBot uses full-text indexing, and it has cataloged every word that appears on more than 110 million documents. Not surprisingly, a full-text index generates a lot of hits. Often, many of these hits aren't pertinent to what you're seeking.

HotBot has bright colors and a bright search engine. You can search by keyword, date, or language, and an **Advanced Search** *allows even more options.*

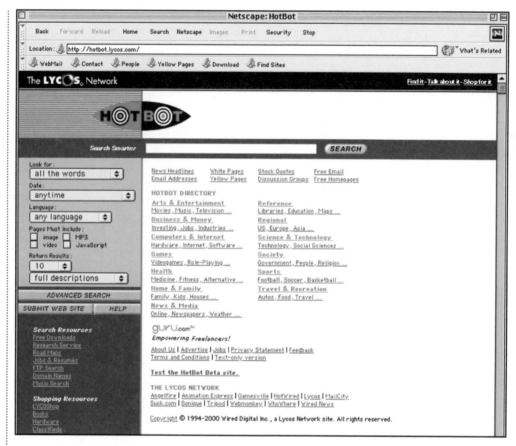

To help you avoid this situation, you can do one of two things: Add more query terms to make your search more specific, or use the pull-down menus to help you focus your search.

For example, if you're looking for "last-minute travel bargains," enter that phrase rather than just "travel bargains." To help you fine-tune the results even more, you can use one of the pull-down menus, such as the one that allows you to sort the results by date.

In addition, HotBot's home page contains a directory. If you search by directory, HotBot will help you narrow your search quickly. For example, say you wanted to research a potential investment. You would select **Business & Money** to view an alphabetical list of all the information in this category. Notice HotBot contains links to several databases, including a direct link to Hoover's so you can research your investment.

To conduct a detailed search, click on **Advanced Search**. A menu of options will appear. Among these options is a word filter, which allows you to limit your search results to Web pages that contain, or don't contain, the words in your query.

Also of interest is a **word stemming** option, which searches for grammatical variations of words in your query. For example, if "thought" is one of the words in your query, HotBot also will find words such as "think" and "thinking."

Finally, if you get into the **Advanced Search** option and decide that you're being too specific, you can revise your search, choose fewer options, or start over entirely.

FAST FACTS ABOUT HOTBOT

- Allows you to construct a complex query
- Contains many pull-down menus that provide options for narrowing your search
- Allows you to fine-tune a search by adding more words
- Has an advanced option for word stemming, which allows you to search for grammatical variations of a search term

OTHER WAYS TO SEARCH THE WEB

In addition to these popular search sites, the Web contains several **metasearch engines** that take one query and send it to several major search sites and then display the results. An example of a metasearch engine is MetaCrawler *(www.go2net.com)*, which is part of the Go2Net Network.

Using a metasearch engine has advantages and disadvantages. A metasearch engine may save you time because several different search engines are queried at once. The big disadvantage, however, is that you must enter your query in the simplest format possible because no standardization exists between the various search engines.

If you want very specific information, the Web also contains several specialized search engines that can help you. Some of these include:

- OneLook Dictionaries *(www.onelook.com)*—Gives users access to hundreds of online dictionaries

- MapQuest *(www.mapquest.com)*—Provides door-to-door directions to any business or residence in the United States, and provides maps of several international cities

- News Index *(www.newsindex.com)*—Lets you search more than 300 news sources around the world

◗ The Lawguru.com *(www.lawguru.com)*—Searches for codes, statutes, and other legal information

FINDING FRIENDS

The Web contains a wealth of information and many databases that can be used to find someone. Here are a few sites to check out.

• Investigative Links 2000 *(http://www.pimall.com/nais/links. html#anchor3541819)*. This site is a good place to begin your search, because it contains an extensive index of searchable Web databases.

• Switchboard *(www.switchboard.com)*. This site contains a directory of all listed phone numbers in the United States, along with corresponding addresses. Switchboard even allows you to search for a person's e-mail address, and it provides door-to-door directions to businesses and residences within the United States. To locate a person, enter their first and last names in Switchboard's search engine. Within seconds, Switchboard will display a list of possible matches. (Detective's tip: If you're looking for a woman, only enter her last name, since women often use their initials, rather than their full name, in the phone directory.)

• ClassMates and PlanetAll *(www.classmates.com* and *www.planetall.com)*. Both of these sites are designed to help you find people who share your alma mater, and each has many members. Classmates specializes in helping find high school chums. However, information has its price: Classmates charges $25 for a 24-month membership. PlanetAll, on the other hand, is free. This site contains a database that allows users to search for high school and college friends, or former business associates. If you locate the person you're seeking, PlanetAll then e-mails them to see if they'll agree to exchange personal information with you.

• Yahoo! People Search *(people.yahoo.com)*. This site lets you search by name, domain, city, or state to find that elusive person's e-mail, phone number, and address. Yahoo! People Search also gives users the option of creating a profile that lists their marital status, occupation, e-mail address, and hobbies.

Seek and You Shall Find • 45

Browsers, such as Microsoft Internet Explorer, also have jumped on the search-tool bandwagon. To activate this feature in Microsoft Internet Explorer, click on the **Search** button in the Menu bar, and Microsoft will link you to AltaVista's search engine.

FEELING OVERWHELMED?

At this point, you're either feeling much better about finding things on the Web, or you're ready to stand up and fling this book across the room. If you're feeling just a bit overwhelmed, remind yourself that searching the Web isn't a science, it's an art.

Searching is one of the most interactive aspects of the Web. You choose which search tool to use, how you will use it, and which search results you want to view. That's why two people searching for information about the same topic can get very different results.

The results of a search often reflect the way you reason and may even reflect your personal interests. This medium can be as interesting and exciting as you want it to be. Remember that you drive each Web search, and you ultimately determine where you'll stop on the Information Superhighway.

HINTS FOR BETTER HITS

Given the enormous amount of information on the Internet, it's a wonder that anybody can find anything. Conducting an efficient Web search doesn't have to be difficult, however. Here are a few tips that can help you conduct a better search.

- Use several search tools. Every search tool uses a different method to index items on the Web. Some search by keyword or concept; others search by subject. Consequently, the same query will generate different results among various search tools. A thorough searcher uses several tools.

- Know which search tool to use. For general topics, product searches, and information on current events, it's best to use a directory, such as Yahoo! *(www.yahoo.com)*. If you're researching a specialized topic or subject, use a search engine such as InfoSeek *(www.infoseek.com)* or Excite *(www.excite.com)*.

▶ Find a search tool that works for you—whether it's a directory or a search engine—and learn its advanced features. Remember that some search tips work better with one search tool than another.

▶ Keep it simple at first. Avoid searching for obscure information that won't likely be found unless you use a sophisticated search method. Master a few simple searches before tackling complex ones.

▶ Be specific. If you've got more hits than you can shake a stick at, narrow your search by using unusual keywords that clearly identify the topic you're seeking. If you can't think of the word you want, try using a synonym.

▶ Try to sort by date. If you're looking for news and other time-sensitive material, see if the search tool you're using will allow you to sort the results by date of publication.

▶ Word order matters. Enter the most important concept first. If you're looking for information on U.S. senators, enter "U.S. senators" rather than "senators U.S."

▶ Remember that many search tools are case sensitive. A lower-case search string will pull up both lower-case and uppercase matches. The reverse, however, is not true. Don't use capital letters unless the term you're looking for is a proper noun that is always capitalized.

▶ Pay attention to relevance. OK, so your query returned 200 hits. Chances are the more useful hits will be listed on the first two pages. Search engines such as Excite have a "relevance indicator" that ranks each hit, so be sure to make good use of it.

▶ Learn the logic. Most search programs use Boolean logic, which allows you to expand or limit a query by using quotes and words like "AND" and "OR." (Note: Words such as "AND" or "OR" should always be entered in all capital letters in the query box. This signals the search engine to exclude those words from the search.) For example, the query John AND Smith or "John Smith" returns documents with both

words. John OR Smith and John Smith both retrieve documents with either word, not necessarily both. Other Boolean operators, or words that modify the way a search engine handles a string of words, include a plus sign or a minus sign. Put a + symbol in front of words that must be included in the search results and a - symbol in front of the words that should be excluded from the search results. For example, if you want to search for dogs for sale, but not puppies, you could enter dogs+adult-puppies.

- Use a wildcard character, such as an asterisk, when the word you're seeking might have several endings. For example, the query **boat*** on AltaVista will return information on boats, boaters, boating, etc.

- Eliminate unnecessary words. Don't include words such as "a," "an," or "the" in a query.

- Always check for misspelled words. If you're not getting any results, check to make sure your query is spelled correctly.

OUR BEST INTERNET SITES

Now that you know how to perform a successful search, it's time to start exploring the Web. We recommend starting with the sites we've reviewed in the following chapters. The Web-site reviews in this book cover topics of interest to seniors, such as health, finances, and travel. They are some of the best sites you can find online.

Choosing the topics for each chapter, and deciding which Web sites would be profiled, wasn't easy. Below you will find a description of the content and criteria used to select each Web site profiled in chapters 5 through 12.

Chapter 5: Sites for Seniors. This chapter contains a good mix of Web sites from the nonprofit, government, and commercial sectors. Many of the Web sites in this section have won industry awards, and all of them contain useful information specifically for seniors.

These Web sites are well organized, easy to navigate, and easy to read; many sites use a larger-than-average typeface. Each Web site also contains links to other Web resources of interest to seniors.

Chapter 6: Shopping. Shopping is a popular online activity. In recent years, Internet shopping has received a lot of press—both good and bad. The sites profiled in this chapter were selected with the utmost care. Each is well respected within the Web community and by the consumers who use them. Although these sites use different methods to make online shopping more efficient, each site uses the best Internet security protocols available to protect and secure customers' transactions.

Specific sites, such as PlanetRx and Peapod, were included because they demonstrate how a number of online shopping sites sell a wide range of merchandise. The number of cyberservices available to consumers undoubtedly will grow in the future as more people start using the Web to conduct everyday activities.

Chapter 7: Health. The Web sites in this chapter were selected based on the reliability and timeliness of the information they provide. Included in this section are health topics of special interest to seniors, such as diabetes. However, most of the sites profiled cover a wide range of health and fitness issues.

Many of these sites have received awards from the Internet community, while others are well-regarded by members of the medical community. In addition, many of the sites in this section subscribe to the HONcode principles from the Health on the Net Foundation, which is working to improve the quality of health-care information available on the Internet.

Chapter 8: Travel. A few years ago, computerized reservation systems could only be accessed by a travel agent. Thanks to the Web, you now can gain access to much of this information yourself and act as your own travel agent. Each site in this section reflects the travel interests and needs of seniors. Some sites, such as Microsoft Expedia, were chosen because of the broad range of services they provide travelers. Others, such as BedandBreakfast.com, reflect how travelers' special interests are finding their way onto the Web. All of the sites covered in this chapter, however, accomplish a common goal of communicating pertinent information and guiding visitors through the online reservation process.

Chapter 9: Financial Resources. Like the Health chapter, the Web sites in this section were chosen based on the reliability and timeliness of the information they provide. A wide range of online financial resources can be found here. You can find out how to start and manage your own online portfolio, trade stocks online, research a company you might invest in, or read what financial experts and successful investors have to say about various investment strategies.

Chapter 10: Hobbies. Popularity played a major role in determining what Web sites would be profiled in this section. Genealogy is a very popular hobby, particularly among seniors. You can also find Web sites that cover decorating and cooking. Pet lovers will also find plenty of information about how to keep their pets healthy and happy. Each site in this chapter is easy to navigate. These sites also contain links to other excellent resources on the Web.

Chapter 11: Entertainment. Like the entries in the Hobbies chapter, these sites are very popular among seniors who like to enjoy their free time. There are easy-to-use and informative sites containing just about everything you'd like to know about movies and computer games. And sports fans are sure to love the detailed, up-to-the-minute coverage they will find on the Web. We've chosen the most comprehensive sites so you're never left searching for stats about your favorite teams or your favorite actors!

Chapter 12: News and Weather. In general, seniors read more and take more interest in current events than other age groups. The Web sites profiled in this section cover a broad range of reliable news sources, including online newspapers and interactive news channels.

The two Web sites that cover the weather complement each other. Each contains features not found at the other site, and both are highly rated.

CHAPTER 5
Sites for Seniors

ACCESS AMERICA FOR SENIORS

www.seniors.gov

E-mail: Varies by government agency.

Access America for Seniors is a one-stop shop for getting government information. You can find information ranging from an estimate of your Social Security benefits to a comparison of nursing homes or Medicare options.

An alphabetical list of federal agencies that provide services to seniors appears on the home page. The home page also shows information broken down into general categories, such as **Benefits**. This feature is particularly helpful if you're not sure which federal agency has the information you're seeking.

The top and left sides of each page on the Web site contain navigational tools. These navigational tools allow you to jump from information source to information source within the site. A box in the lower left corner contains a list of hyperlinks that will whisk you to a variety of different federal Web sites. When linking to a federal agency, a screen appears telling visitors they're leaving the Access America for Seniors Web site. While some users may find this screen helpful in terms of navigation, others may feel it borders on overkill—particularly after you've figured out that the screen will appear every time you link to a federal agency.

Visitors who are seeking information on a specific subject will benefit from Access America's internal search engine. The search engine, which is powered by InfoSeek, gives you the option of searching only the site's contents for information or expanding the search to include the entire Internet.

A **Help** link, which is located just below the search engine's query box, gives users some quick tips and examples of how to conduct an effective search. New Web users will find this feature particularly helpful, because the methods used to conduct a search vary by search engine.

The site also contains an **Ask Us/Tell Us** link. This is helpful if you're not sure which government agency can answer your question. You can complete an

online question form, and Access America for Seniors will forward the form to the appropriate government agency. That agency will then respond to your question via e-mail.

Finally, if your computer's modem runs slowly or is out-of-date, choose the **Text Only** option, which can be found in the upper left corner of the home page. Choosing the **Text Only** option speeds up your search, because you won't have to wait for your modem to load pictures and other graphics.

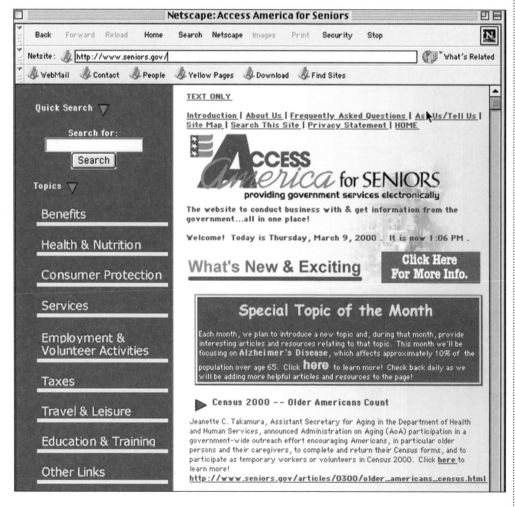

Along the left side of the Access America for Seniors home page is a list of topics. You can link to any of these if you're just browsing, or perform a quick search for specific information in the box above.

AARP WEBPLACE

www.aarp.org

E-mail: member@aarp.org

Visitors to this site can find everything they ever wanted to know about the American Association of Retired Persons (AARP), the nation's largest organization for people 50 and older. This self-promoting site contains lots of links to the vast array of services and benefits offered by the association.

Unlike other Web sites, AARP's Webplace doesn't inundate visitors with too many graphics, hyperlinks, or obtrusive ads, and the site is visually pleasing. Hyperlinks to vital information can be found in the navigation bar, and subjects of interest to seniors are listed by category.

Three categories at this site—**Computers/Internet, Health and Wellness**, and **Legislative Issues**—are particularly good. Sandy Berger's **Computer & Technology** section is aimed toward intelligent novices, and you can find links here to computer hardware reviews, computer user tips, software reviews, Web-site reviews, and more.

The **Health and Wellness** section is divided into subcategories, and links to caregiver resources, community resources, health insurance options, Medicare, nursing home information, and more can be found. Before leaving the **Health and Wellness** section, be sure to check out the **Explore Health** link. It is loaded with interesting feature articles and contains links to some valuable member benefits, such as the AARP Pharmacy Service.

AARP's Webplace also does a good job of organizing information about legislative issues that are being addressed by the association. Visitors can find information on issues affecting seniors, such as Social Security, Medicare, managed care, utility restructuring, and tax reform.

If you don't care much about tax reform and politics, why not go shopping? Simply click on the **Shop** link in the navigational bar. AARP has researched some cybershops to make sure they are legitimate and provide adequate security for online transactions.

It's easy to start linking about willy-nilly when you visit AARP's Webplace. If you can't remember what brought you to the site in the first place, find the **Home** link on the navigational bar, and click on it to go back to the home page.

Once you're at the home page, regroup by using one of two search devices. A **Quick Search** engine on the home page allows you to search by using a keyword or phrase. There's also a **Quick Finder** pull-down menu, which lists some of the more commonly referenced topics that can be found at the site.

Before leaving the **Health and Wellness** *section, be sure to check out the* **Explore Health** *link, which contains feature articles, discussions, tools for staying healthy, and a list of member-health services sponsored by AARP.*

SENIORCOM

www.senior.com

E-mail: support@senior.com

All the information at this award-winning Web site is specifically geared to people aged 50 or older. Visitors can find information on subjects such as computing, entertainment, health, money, relationships, and more.

On the home page are several short news items. Each news item has an accompanying hyperlink that, when clicked on, will transport you to the text of the entire article.

The left side of the home page contains a list of **Channels**, or links, that connect you to specific categories of information. You can link to topics such as elder care, doctors, health news, and estate planning. You can also find links to chat rooms, forums, clubs, and other places where you can meet people.

If you want to visit one of SeniorCom's chat rooms, join an online club, or use other services provided by this site, you must register. Luckily, registration is free and easy to do. To register, just click on the words **Free Membership** in the upper left corner to get to SeniorCom's membership registration form. (Tip: Rather than use your mouse to move from field to field within the registration form, use the Tab key on your keyboard.)

Many Web sites with free information encourage visitors to register with them. Some Web sites will sell this registration information to advertisers. If you're concerned about this, be sure to read the Web site's **Privacy Statement**. At SeniorCom, visitors who register can indicate whether or not they would like to receive any mail from advertisers.

The second reason many Web sites like folks to register is that it allows them to tailor your experience at their site. Most Web sites do this by using a "cookie," which is one of the technological features provided by your browser. For example, when you visit SeniorCom, the site contacts your browser and the browser creates and stores a cookie on your computer. This cookie remembers the information you accessed when visiting the site.

Once the cookie is set, the cookie will "recognize" you the next time you visit the site. This process takes place instantly, and it allows the Web site to load information and advertisements that may be of interest to you based on the things you accessed during your last visit.

Contrary to rumor, cookie files can't access personal information stored on your computer's hard drive and use it to wreak havoc in your life. Cookies can only collect the information you supply when you visit a Web site.

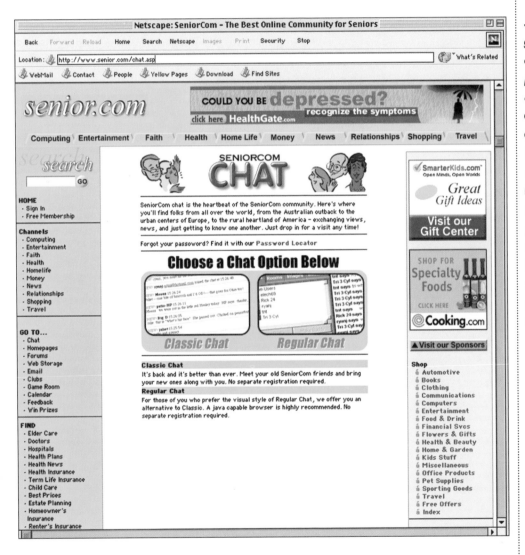

SeniorCom gives visitors two chat room program options: **Classic Chat** *or* **Regular Chat**. *If you're a Web newcomer, choose the* **Regular Chat** *option. This chat program is more up-to-date, and it looks similar to the chat programs used at other Web sites.*

ThirdAge

www.thirdage.com

E-mail: feedback@thirdage.com

"ThirdAge (thurd'aj): (n.) 1. A time of life characterized by happiness, freedom, and learning. 2. A life stage following 'youth' and preceding 'old age.' 3. A Web site where like-minded people find intelligent conversations and useful tools. 4. Your best years yet!"

That's how this Web site defines itself and those who visit it. Mary Furlong, Ed.D., founded ThirdAge's Web site in 1996. Furlong also founded SeniorNet, the first online community for older adults. Like SeniorNet, ThirdAge gives mature adults a medium for sharing their knowledge with each other.

ThirdAge's Web site is arranged like a subject tree with broad topics divided into progressively smaller subtopics. General topics include **Computers**, **Family & Pets**, **Health**, **Money**, **News & Views**, **Love & Sex**, **Politics**, and **Travel**.

Once you link to a general topic, you can begin focusing your search by linking to one of several subtopics. For example, after linking to the general topic **News & Views**, you can link to subcategories on **Archives**, **Newsletters**, **Top Stories**, and **Your Opinion.**

Every general topic page also contains several pull-down menus. These pull-down menus contain links to tutorials, subject guides, tools, features, forums, and other Web sites with pertinent information.

If you're looking to make friends online, ThirdAge provides plenty of opportunities to do so. Visitors can link to an online community, chat room, or forum that allows users to post their thoughts on various subjects. You also can sign up for an online class or join an e-mail circle.

Visitors who really want to keep abreast of the latest news can sign up to receive one of the site's many online newsletters. These newsletters cover topics ranging from travel bargains to sexual vitality. In fact, ThirdAge's **Love & Sex** category is very popular. Visitors to this section can find straight talk about how to have a satisfying sex life and maintain a healthy outlook on romance. Of interest is Dr. David Schnarch's **Intimate Lives Forum**, which allows ThirdAgers to post questions and comments on sex, love, and intimate adult relationships.

Web newcomers also should spend a few minutes surfing around ThirdAge's **Computers** category. This category contains links to several free computer classes you can take via the Internet.

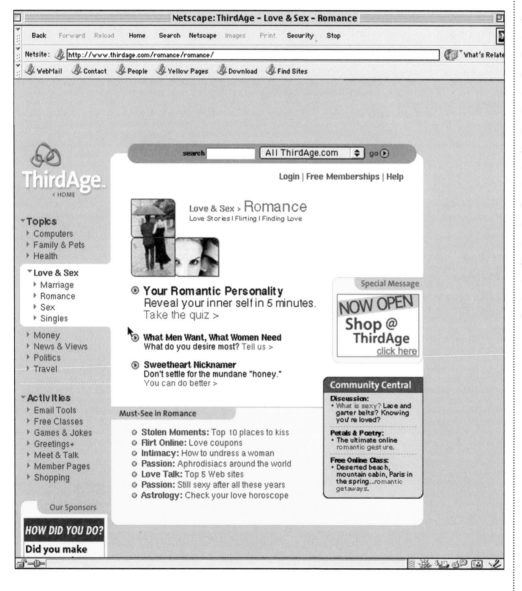

*Although not immediately apparent, the subcategories for each topic are listed just beneath each general topic. For example, when the **Love & Sex** box is highlighted, it reveals subcategories on marriage, romance, sex, and singles.*

ELDERWEB

www.elderweb.com

E-mail: info@elderweb.com

If you want to see what a well-organized Web site looks like, visit ElderWeb. This award-winning site makes accessing information easy. The home page's layout is straightforward and uncluttered. Visitors can find links to main topics of information, as well as the organization's street address, phone number, toll-free FAX number, and e-mail address.

Putting this information on the home page, and every Web page throughout this site, makes it easy for visitors to contact the organization should they have a question or comment. Given the nature of the material you can find at Elder-Web, you may very well have a question.

This site contains more than 4,500 links to information on long-term care options, as well as an expanding library of articles, reports, news, and events. Some of this information is geared toward professionals, but much of it is written for regular folks who need to make some tough decisions.

When you first visit ElderWeb, you might want to begin by linking to the **Site Map**, which gives an overview of the site's structure and content. The site contains a good internal search engine, as well as two other search engines powered by Excite. These additional engines allow you to expand your search to include the entire Web or Excite's news archive.

Most of the information on this site is arranged by subject, state, or region. This makes things convenient because much of the information about elder care resources varies by state or region. In some cases, you can search for local information by entering your ZIP code.

If you're looking for links to long-term care facilities, click on the **Regional Information** link, and then link to **Eldercare Directories**. This is a great place to get an idea about what is available in your area.

Once you've done that, link to **Finance & Law**. This section contains a number of valuable resources and information about ways to pay for long-term care. Like other Web sites, ElderWeb is open 24 hours a day. If you don't have enough time to call an organization or agency for information during regular business hours, or you're up late one night trying to evaluate your options, visit ElderWeb. This site succeeds in its goal of imparting as much direct information as possible.

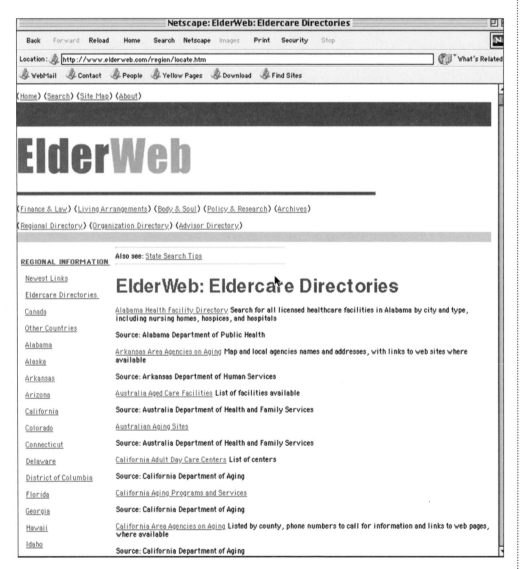

If you're looking for a doctor or a long-term care facility, link to **Regional Information** and then link to **Eldercare Directories**. Here you'll find links to retirement facilities, a nursing home locator, a directory of adult day care centers, and more.

AGENET

www.agenet.com

E-mail: webmaster@agenet.com

Both seniors and caregivers can find a wealth of information about geriatric issues at AgeNet. There are links to legal, insurance, and financial information, as well as a handy list of products designed to help seniors.

One of the better categories at this site is **Geriatric Health**. This category contains information about diabetes, Alzheimer's disease, Parkinson's disease, depression in the elderly, stroke, arthritis, osteoporosis, aging and exercise, and more.

Adult children caring for an aging parent are sure to find the **Caregiver Support** and **Housing/Living Alternatives** links useful as well. You can even access a database that will allow you to search for a geriatric care manager by state. Geriatric care managers, a rapidly growing professional group, monitor an elderly family member, help older adults plan and coordinate their daily living activities, and help them communicate with their relatives on a regular basis, regardless of where they live. Other links that are exceptionally good include one that allows visitors to read about the 200 most commonly prescribed medications for older adults and another that summarizes the advantages and disadvantages of implementing a reverse mortgage.

Several noted authors have advice columns on AgeNet. Harriet Sarnoof Schiff, author of *Living Through Mourning* and *The Bereaved Parent*, writes a column on how to deal with death and dying. Dr. David L. Cram, author of *The Healing Touch*, has a regular column that deals with health and health care issues.

Like many other Web sites, AgeNet asks visitors to register with the site. Registration is free and allows registrants to access AgeNet's **Chat and Message Board** areas and receive advance information regarding issues and solutions that are important to seniors.

AgeNet also helps link seniors to some valuable services they might need. For example, older adults who are concerned about the potential adverse reaction to prescription and over-the-counter drugs can pay $45 to get a comprehensive assessment of their medications done by a pharmacist. Other services that are provided for a fee include creating an online will or signing up for an online

medication reminder service. Not all the links deal with serious topics, though. You may want to check out the list of celebrities who are 50 and older to see if you share your birthday with your favorite actor or actress.

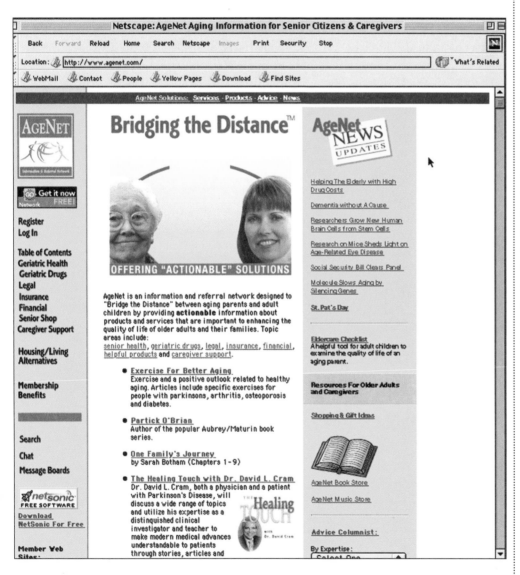

AgeNet contains links to many valuable resources of interest to both seniors and their children. Visitors can find links to information about living wills and estate planning, making out an online will, or searching for a lawyer that specializes in elder law.

SENIORNET

www.seniornet.com

E-mail: Varies by department.

SeniorNet was founded in 1986 to promote the use of computer technology to enhance the lives of seniors. Today more than 32,000 people aged 50 and older belong to this national nonprofit organization.

This Web site provides a lot of free information and services to visitors, whether or not they are members. However, you may want to join this organization to take advantage of some members-only perks that can be found both online and offline.

SeniorNet has more than 160 learning centers located throughout the United States. These centers offer a low-cost, friendly introduction to computers. The curriculum is composed of introductory computer courses that explain word processing, spreadsheets, and going online and using the Internet. More advanced courses cover topics such as genealogy, graphics, personal financial management, and tax preparation using a computer.

Many centers offer open lab time to students, and classes are taught and coached by volunteer instructors, many of whom are senior citizens themselves. Peer instruction has proven effective, and to date more than 90,000 people have taken a class through a SeniorNet Learning Center.

In addition to computer training, SeniorNet and IBM have a program that provides seniors with discounted computer systems and software programs. To get more detailed information on this program, click on the **Marketplace** link on SeniorNet's home page.

While computer shopping, take note of the **Support** and **Download** icons located in the upper right corner of each IBM/SeniorNet Purchase Program shopping page. These icons link visitors to IBM's online support center or to IBM's software archive, which contains thousands of free software programs that visitors can download.

SeniorNet also has several links to some good informational newsletters. These newsletters contain computing tips, stories about seniors' attitudes about and perceptions of computers and the Internet, and announcements of new learning centers that are opening around the country.

This site also gives members an opportunity to showcase their work. The **SeniorNet Showcase** contains exhibits that describe various computer and

online-supported projects, an art gallery, and profiles of some of SeniorNet's more interesting members.

SeniorNet is one of those Web sites you might want to bookmark—particularly if you believe in lifelong education. It seems like something interesting is always going on at SeniorNet, whether it's a new discussion group or a new piece of digital art that has been posted at the site by a senior.

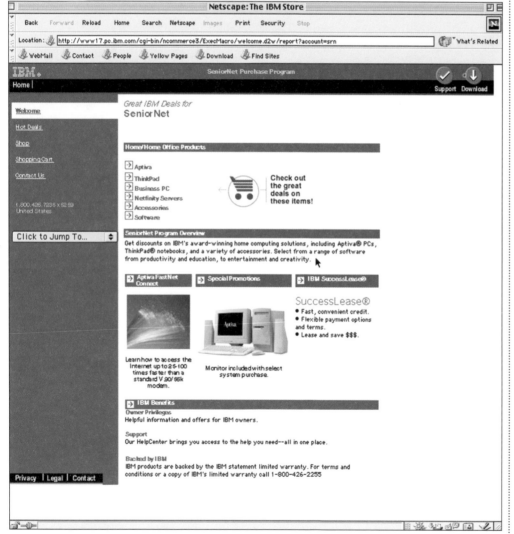

This screen shows the SeniorNet Purchase Program for buying home computers. The site has teamed with IBM to offer this service to its users. Reviews and information of the computers listed are available by clicking on each computer's name. Special deals are listed, and customer service is available by phone using the toll-free number on the left side of the screen.

SENIORS-SITE

www.seniors-site.com

E-mail: writers@seniors-site.com

Seniors-Site illustrates just how much people aged 50 and older have embraced new technology and the Web. Walter J. Cheney, 70, is the Webmaster for this site, and the topics and services you'll find here reflect many of the interests, opinions, and issues of importance to older Americans.

Not all of the information, however, is geared toward seniors. Visitors also can find informative links aimed at seniors' children, grandchildren, and caregivers. This is a good site to visit if you want to share your knowledge, thoughts, and experiences. For example, a computer specialist, veterinarian, counselor, therapeutic caregiver, and variety of other professionals form a network of online resources. These folks have agreed to provide free advice to seniors who contact them via e-mail.

The variety of message boards at this site is impressive. Visitors can post messages and share information with each other on topics ranging from grandparenting to reverse mortgages. There's even a link to help those who are seeking an online pen pal. Unfortunately, this site doesn't contain an internal search engine, and the **Site Map**, while comprehensive, uses a smaller font that some visitors might find a little difficult to read. Still, you probably should begin your tour by going to the **Site Map**, which lists the site's information and shows how it's organized.

You'll find links to topics such as frauds, scams and abuses, physical ailments, alternative medicine, housing options, grandparenting resources, information about pets, and poems and prose. Undoubtedly **Funstuff and humor** is one of the more frequently accessed links. If you're in the mood to read a new joke or share your own, this is the place to visit. Visitors also might want to check out the unbelievable collection of tombstone epitaphs sent in by seniors.

Seniors also can find information about more serious subjects, such as how to handle loneliness. There are also links to information that can help widows and widowers and those coping with a chronic illness.

Finally, remember that it's buyer beware when it comes to purchasing products or services advertised on the Internet. Visitors can find a number of advertisements for various products and services at Seniors-Site. However, the presence of an ad doesn't necessarily mean Seniors-Site endorses the product or service.

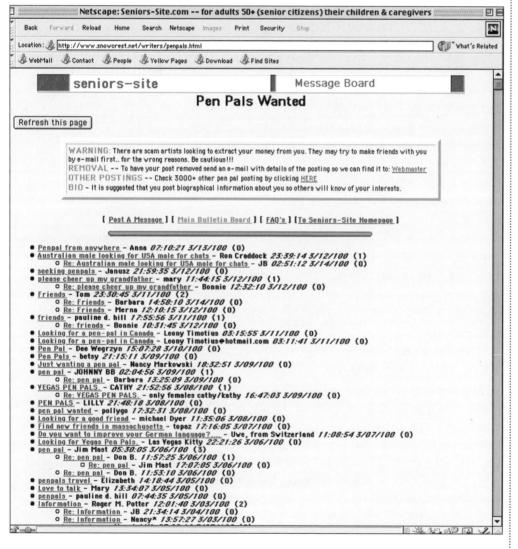

Seniors-Site contains an online bulletin board for seniors who are looking for an online pen pal. The site contains thousands of listings from folks located throughout the United States.

AMERICA'S GUIDE

www.americasguide.com

E-mail: info@americasguide.com

America's Guide organizes information of interest to seniors into a subject directory. Visitors can find information on health and wellness, discount programs for seniors, community resources, finances and financial planning, housing, and travel and leisure.

Of particular interest is the site's **Resource Directory**, which helps link seniors to thousands of businesses and facilities offering products and services. You can browse an alphabetized list of organizations, such as acute care facilities, and then search by state or city for locations in your area.

Like many Web sites, America's Guide encourages visitors to register. Registration is free, and membership gives you access to benefits such as posting a message on one of the Web site's many message boards. Membership also gives you access to a personal organizer of information.

When you're a member and you use the site's **Resource Directory**, you will see a green button labeled **Request** next to each business listing. If you are interested in a particular business or facility, you can click on the **Request** button, and America's Guide will process your request and pass the information along. This service saves you time because you don't have to contact the business directly.

If you're afraid the request process will open you up to an onslaught of junk e-mail, click on the **Help** link to read more about this site's privacy policy. America's Guide states that it does not sell or share e-mail addresses or any other visitor information with third parties, and e-mail addresses and other volunteered information is kept confidential.

Once you've requested information from a business or facility, your request is placed in a personal organizer. Your personal organizer has a pull-down menu, with options such as **Received info**, **Interested**, **Not interested**, and **Remove from list**, that will allow you to track the status of each of your requests.

Finally, before leaving this site, check out the **News & Information** category. You'll find a list of links to magazines for seniors that cover subjects such as golf, retirement, fitness, gardening, health and medicine, puzzles, cooking, and travel. Within this category you also can find links to get the national news, a local weather report, or see what's going on in your state government.

If you should run across a term you're not familiar with while reading a news item of interest, back up to the main **News & Information** page and access the site's interactive glossary. The interactive glossary defines many terms used to describe the ever-increasing range of services and products being offered in the geriatric field.

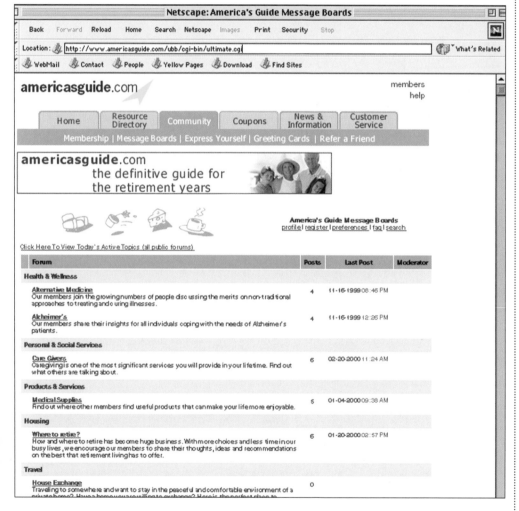

America's Guide contains many message boards. Although visitors can access information posted on a message board, you can't post a message unless you complete the site's free membership registration form.

NATIONAL SENIOR SERVICE CORPS

www.seniorcorps.org

E-mail: nsscjoin@cns.gov

Many seniors volunteer their time and expertise to community projects. If you're considering volunteering your time and want to know what opportunities are available in your area, check out the National Senior Service Corps' Web site.

Nearly half a million Americans aged 55 and older have served in the National Senior Service Corps. The Corps runs three programs: the Foster Grandparent Program, the Senior Companion Program, and the Retired and Senior Volunteer Program (RSVP).

The Foster Grandparent Program pairs seniors with children who need their help and guidance. The Senior Companion Program links seniors to other older adults in their community who need assistance. The third program, RSVP, allows seniors to take part in a wide variety of community projects, many of which have been started by other National Senior Service Corps volunteers.

If you're like most people, you would like to know what will be expected of you as a volunteer. The National Senior Service Corps Web site contains answers to many questions frequently asked by prospective volunteers. You can read detailed descriptions of each of the three main programs, get an estimate of the time you'll spend each week doing volunteer work, and learn what you'll need to do to become a volunteer.

The National Senior Service Program is one of several programs administered by the Corporation for National Service. The corporation also oversees AmeriCorps, America Reads, and several other programs that you can link to from the National Senior Service Corps Web site.

To get a quick overview of the many volunteer programs administered by the Corporation for National Service, click on the **State Profiles** link on the home page, and then link to your state to find a list of volunteer programs that are already underway. This section contains stories about some volunteers' experiences, and you can find a list of people to contact when you're ready to get started.

Finally, be sure to check out links to Senior Service Corps' partners in service. Of interest to seniors are the links to the Points of Light Foundation, which is working to help solve serious social problems, and America's Promise, which is working to build and strengthen the character of today's youth.

Netscape: Corporation for National Service: Senior Corps!

| Back | Forward | Reload | Home | Search | Netscape | Images | Print | Security | Stop |

Location: http://www.seniorcorps.org/   What's Relate

WebMail | Contact | People | Yellow Pages | Download | Find Sites

 Corporation for National Service

 SENIOR CORPS

Information about Becoming Involved
How you can make a difference by serving with a Foster Grandparent, RSVP, or Senior Companion Program
Partners in Service with the Senior Corps
How your organization can get involved
Resources for Programs
What project directors, staff, sponsors, commissions, state offices, and other Senior Corps folks need to know
President's Student Service Challenge
Honors and scholarships for young people who serve their communities
Research Materials
The history of the Senior Corps, facts and figures, and more
Employment, Fellowships, and Internships
Job, fellowship, and internship listings and information
State Profiles **New List Item**
Find out how Senior Corps, AmeriCorps, and Learn and Serve: America made a difference in your state
Senior Corps News
Senior Corps Updates, Press releases, National Service News, and more.

Please send comments or questions regarding this site to the webmaster

Contact Information | Privacy Policy

This is the Senior Corps!
Through the National Senior Service Corps, nearly half a million Americans age 55 and older share their time and talents to help their communities.

Related Service Programs

AMERICORPS
LEARN AND SERVE
AMERICA READS

Newsflash!
Draft Project Director Handbooks for Review

MLK Day of Service

New! - Senior Corps Updates

Related Websites

Subscribe Today to the
NSSCtalk **Listserv**
Take a look at what else is available from the National Service Resource Center

Access America The website for seniors to conduct business with and get information from the government all in one place.

The home page of the National Senior Service Corps contains links to a variety of volunteer programs of interest to seniors, as well other service programs administered by the Corporation for National Service.

Chapter 6
Shopping

YAHOO! SHOPPING

http://shopping.yahoo.com

E-mail: Click on the Feedback link located near the bottom of select Web pages.

Yahoo! (yes, it is spelled with an exclamation point) is not only a searchable subject directory, it's also a Web portal that offers visitors a variety of services, including links to many different online shops. Online shoppers can access Yahoo! Shopping by linking to it from the Yahoo! home page *(www.yahoo.com)* or by typing in its direct Web address *(http://shopping.yahoo.com)*.

This mega-shopping site has a little something for everyone—especially seniors. On the home page, visitors will notice that online shops have been divided into several categories, such as apparel, accessories, and shoes; art and collectibles; bath and beauty; books; flowers, gifts, and occasions; food and beverages; home and garden; health and wellness; movies and video; and travel.

The home page also contains links to some popular **Hot Products**, such as Pokémon and DVD players. Shoppers who want to know what others are buying can link to see a sample of the items purchased on Yahoo! during the previous hour.

The lower left corner of the home page contains a list of resources for shoppers. You can create a gift registry for yourself, view a friend's registry, and apply for a Yahoo! VISA card online.

If you plan to do a lot of shopping, you might want to set up a **Yahoo! Wallet**. To set up a **Yahoo! Wallet**, you must create a Yahoo! ID, choose a personal security key or password, and then enter your name, shipping address, and credit card information. Yahoo! then stores this information in a secure environment. This expedites future shopping trips, because **Yahoo! Wallet** holders don't have to enter this information every time they buy an item at a store affiliated with Yahoo! Instead, they can access their online wallet and Yahoo! does the rest.

Yahoo! also provides an interesting shopping service called **Yahoo! Points**. Frequent online shoppers can accumulate points through Yahoo! Shopping and later redeem these points for gifts. To help first-time visitors get started, Yahoo! gives 300 points just for signing up.

If it sounds like Yahoo! makes online shopping easy, remember that's their goal. Yahoo! wants you to visit their shopping site and keep coming back. When it comes to e-commerce, attracting shoppers is the name of the game.

Netscape: Yahoo! Wallet

Back | Forward | Reload | Home | Search | Netscape | Images | Print | Security | Stop

Location: https://edit.secure.yahoo.com/config/wallet_signup?.src=shp&.done=http%3a//shopping.yahoo.com — What's Related

WebMail | Contact | People | Yellow Pages | Download | Find Sites

YAHOO! WALLET   Yahoo! – Help

Yahoo! Wallet and "Express Check Out"   Return to Yahoo! Shopping

"Express Check Out" is a way to order items quickly and easily in Yahoo! Shopping. In order to use it, you need your very own Yahoo! Wallet. Any purchases you make are billed to the credit card and shipped to the address you saved in your Yahoo! Wallet.

Already have a Yahoo! ID? Sign in now!	Don't have a Yahoo! ID?
Yahoo! ID: [ ] Password: [ ] [Sign in] ☐ Remember my Yahoo! ID and Password (What's this?)	**Sign Up now for a Yahoo! ID and Wallet** save your billing and shipping address and store your credit card.

About Security

- Please read this Security Notice about secure access after December 31, 1999.
- Yahoo! Wallet can only be accessed using a Yahoo! Security Key.
- Data is transmitted securely via SSL encryption.
- Click here for our full Privacy Policy or see more details on security.

Note:
We recommend that you sign out of Yahoo! when you leave your computer.

How do I set up my Yahoo! Wallet?
Complete these 2 steps to sign up for Yahoo! Wallet and to enable Express Check Out:

1. **YAHOO!** ☞   2. 🗂

Sign in to Yahoo!
Use your current Yahoo! ID if you already have one, or sign up and get access to all of Yahoo!'s free personalized services.

Set up your Wallet.
Choose your security key, a personal access code like a PIN, and enter your shipping address and credit card billing information.

What is Yahoo! Wallet?
Yahoo! Wallet is a way to store your purchase information safely and securely. It makes shopping at Yahoo! quick and easy. You can:

- Save shipping and billing address information.
- Store your credit card for future purchases.
- Use it wherever Yahoo! Wallet is accepted.

What is Express Check Out?
Express Check Out offers you a quick and easy check out.

- Save time! Any purchases you make will be:
  ○ shipped to the address saved in your Yahoo! Wallet.
  ○ billed to the credit card saved in your Yahoo! Wallet.
- To use your wallet, just click Express Check Out in the Yahoo! Shopping Cart

---

Yahoo! Wallet *saves your name, shipping address, and credit card information so you don't have to re-enter this information every time you buy something on Yahoo! This information is stored in a secure environment and can only be accessed after entering a secret password called a security key.*

AMAZON.COM

www.amazon.com

E-mail: orders@amazon.com

Amazon.com initially made a name for itself by selling books online. However, this giant online store has branched out and now sells music, DVDs, videos, electronics, software, toys, video games, tools, and building supplies.

Be sure to click on the **Site Guide** when visiting the new and expanded Amazon.com to get an idea of what's contained at the site and how it's organized. Some of Amazon.com's additions include an online auction and a collection of "zShops," where thousands of new, used, and hard-to-find items are sold by both individuals and large retail stores.

The most effective way to plow through the items for sale at the zShops is to narrow your search by category, such as **Clothing & Accessories**. Then use a keyword such as "sweaters" to search within the category.

Purchasing items through a zShop is easy. Each seller has specified an asking price and stated their shipping terms. To buy an item, click **Buy It!**, and Amazon.com will walk you through the steps needed to complete your transaction.

If the seller accepts payments from Amazon.com, you can pay them directly by using the **1-Click Settings** option. This option allows shoppers to store their name, shipping address, shipping preference, and credit card information in a secure environment at Amazon.com. To set up an account, click on the **1-Click Settings** link located at the bottom of any Web page.

Another interesting addition is Amazon.com's new alliance with Sotheby's, an international art auction house. Dubbed Sothebys.Amazon.com, the site is hoping to attract thousands of buyers and sellers of collectibles, general art, and antiques to its global marketplace on the Internet.

Like zShops, the **Auctions** area uses a payment method that differs from the rest of the site. Buyers use an online bidding system called Bid-Click. Bid-Click lets you establish your maximum bid, which is kept private, and works to keep your actual bids as low as possible. If another party beats your initial bid, Bid-Click raises your bid by one single increment more than the challenging bid. This pattern continues until another bidder exceeds your maximum bid, or until you win the auction.

Despite its mammoth size and large inventory of products, Amazon.com has a way of making you feel like you're shopping at a neighborhood store. For

example, whether you're buying a book for yourself or a toy for your grandchild, Amazon.com records your purchase by placing a cookie, or small data file, on your computer. When you revisit the site, Amazon.com reads the cookie, addresses you by name, and automatically generates a list of recommendations based on your previous purchase. Infrequent visitors can sign up to receive future recommendations via e-mail.

Given the variety and service, you'll probably wind up joining the more than 4.5 million customers who have registered for free with this site. Many of these customers registered with Amazon.com when it sold books back in the good old days—which in Internet time means anything that occurred more than a year ago. Indeed, Amazon.com is still a favorite site among both avid and casual readers.

To find an item in one of Amazon.com's zShops, it's best to browse by category and keyword. Buyers then use the pull-down menu shown to sort the results by relevance, date, or price.

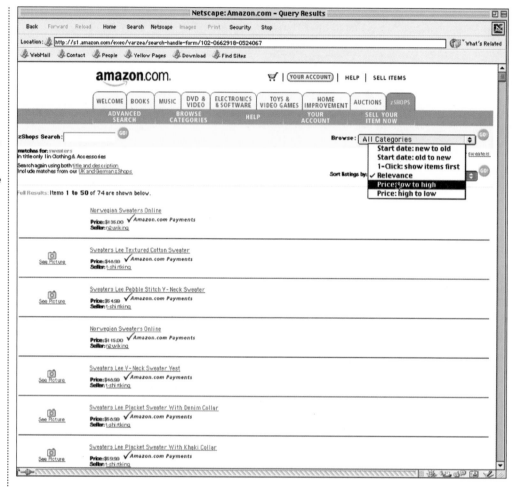

Each book sold by Amazon.com receives a customer star rating and is ranked by sales. The site also provides many interactive features for readers. For example, you can write an online book review, post comments to an online discussion board, create a wish list to share with others, or send an electronic gift certificate or greeting to a friend or loved one. Perks like this give visitors a sense of community. Indeed, Amazon.com manages to personalize the high-tech, online shopping experience.

Purchase circles allow shoppers to see what other people are buying in their state, city, place of business, or alma mater. This screen shows the titles of books favored by Amazon.com shoppers in Clearwater, Florida.

eBay

www.ebay.com

E-mail: For suggestions, suggest@ebay.com; for all other questions, click on the Help link.

This site claims to be the world's first, biggest, and best person-to-person online trading site. Anyone can post an item to sell, and when you visit eBay you will think almost everyone has done so.

Shoppers can find a huge selection of items ranging from antiques to bean-filled toys. eBay holds more than 2.5 million auctions a day that attract buyers and sellers from around the world.

Browsing is free. To find an item, click on **Browse** at the top of any page. Or you can use the site's internal search engine to scour more than 2,500 categories of items.

Those who browse the site or bid on items at eBay aren't charged a fee. However, if you want to sell an item at eBay, you can expect to pay a small fee.

You must register with the site (this service is free) to sell or bid on an item. To post an item, the seller must fill out an online form that contains details about the item to be auctioned and other pertinent information, such as accepted methods of payment and minimum bids.

After completing this form, the seller submits the item, and the bidding begins. Each item is given a number, which allows the seller to track the item's status as the auction progresses.

Buyers, in turn, make their bids by proxy. Potential buyers specify the maximum amounts they wish to bid, which is kept secret. The proxy system automatically places bids for you during the auction, bidding only enough to outbid other bidders. This continues until someone exceeds your maximum bid, the auction ends, or you win the auction. When the auction closes, the seller must contact the winning bidder or bidders within three business days to confirm the final cost and shipping charges and tell them where to send payment.

eBay employs several techniques to help protect buyers and sellers. For starters, there is a **Feedback Forum** where users can post comments about their buying and selling experiences. Second, eBay employs a safety staff called Safe-Harbor. These folks try to prevent fraud, monitor trading offenses, and remove illegal items posted by pranksters.

Finally, every eBay user is protected by insurance free of charge. If you pay for an item and never receive it, or if you receive an item and it's not what you expected, eBay will reimburse you up to $200, less a $25 deductible. Keep this in mind if you plan on buying a higher-priced item. Those bidding on expensive items often use eBay's escrow partner i-Escrow. This escrow company withholds payment to the seller until the buyer has inspected and approved their merchandise. Sellers, in turn, also get an opportunity to inspect and approve a returned item before the buyer gets refunded.

*Check out eBay's **Feedback Forum** before buying or selling online. You'll find comments about the reliability of individual buyers and sellers.*

*Those who like to see what they're buying should check out the **eBay Gallery**, which contains photos of many of the items being auctioned. You also can see the most current bid and the date and time the auction will end.*

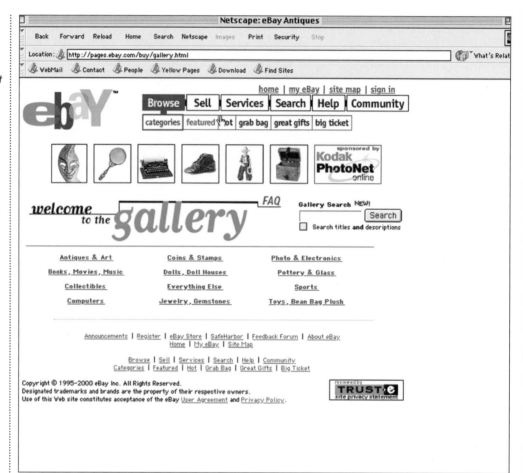

Those who frequent eBay say it is addictive. In fact, the site has an online newsletter and publishes a magazine, which can be found on many newsstands, full of helpful tips and strategies.

One of the better features of this site is that most buyers and sellers are individuals. You won't find many businesses peddling their goods here. This sense of individuality makes eBay's online community one of the liveliest on the Internet, and the site contains many message boards and chat rooms where members can meet and talk. A true member of the community, eBay also is known for holding many auctions where all proceeds are donated to charity.

| File Edit View Go Bookmarks Communicator Help |
| Netscape: eBay item 288448503 (Ends Mar-27-00 00:13:42 PST) – DELAWARE ROLLS "D" MINT QUARTERS |
| Back Forward Reload Home Search Netscape Images Print Security Stop |
| Location: http://cgi.ebay.com/aw-cgi/eBayISAPI.dll?ViewItem&item=288448503 |
| WebMail Contact People Yellow Pages Download Find Sites |

Bidding

DELAWARE ROLLS "D" MINT QUARTERS (Item #288448503)

| Minimum bid | $44.00 |
| **Minimum bid** | **$44.00** |

Please note: your bid is a binding contract.

Quantity you are bidding for

_____

Enter your maximum bid

_____   *Current minimum bid is $44.00*   [review bid]

- This is the amount you are bidding **for each item**.
- *Please take note of the currency in which you are bidding.*
- Remember to type in **numbers only** and use a decimal point (.) when necessary. **Don't include a currency symbol ($) or thousand separator**. For example: 1000000.00
- To finalize your bid, you will need to submit your User ID and Password in the next step — once you click on Review Bid.

This is a Dutch Auction (Multiple Item Auction)!

- For a quick explanation of how this format works, check out Dutch Auction (Multiple Item Auction) guidelines.
- If you've bid on this item before, remember that your new maximum bid total must be **higher** than your previous bid total. Your total is the quantity multiplied by the dollar amount per item you bid.

Your bid is a contract

- Only place a bid if you're serious about buying the item; if you're the winning bidder, you **will** enter into a legally binding contract to purchase the item from the seller.

How to Bid

1. Register if you haven't already. It's free!

2. Read feedback comments left by others about this seller.

3. Read payment and shipping terms, as well as the item description.

4. Contact the seller **before** you bid if you have any questions.

5. **Make a bid!**

You're insured!

Bidding on eBay is done by proxy. You enter the maximum amount you are willing to pay for an item. As the bidding increases, the system automatically increases your bid until the maximum amount you've specified is reached, the auction closes, or you win the auction.

MSN eShop

http://eshop.msn.com

E-mail: Click on the Customer Service link found on any Web page in this site.

Microsoft isn't about to take a back seat when it comes to shopping and e-commerce. At the Microsoft Network (MSN) eShop, you'll find a large selection of products and services for online shoppers.

The MSN eShop home page is well-structured and easy to scan. You'll find a link to daily shopping specials, a shopping search engine, and a gift center where you can purchase gift certificates, create a wish list, or get some suggestions for that special someone who seems to have everything. You'll also find several online shopping guides, including an excellent one for cars and another for women's clothing.

MSN divides its affiliated online shops into categories and subcategories. Some of these cybershops include the **Audio Book Club**, **Beauty.com**, **Cooking.com**, **FTD**, **Garden.com**, **Sears.com**, and **Wine.com**. Of particular interest is the store link to the **Life Extension Foundation**, which claims to be the world's largest organization dedicated to scientific methods of slowing and reversing aging. Here you'll find products you can buy, such as melatonin and DHEA, as well as books of interest to seniors. You also can link to information on health and longevity.

MSN eShop allows visitors and members to sign up to receive a weekly e-mail of shopping specials. You also can link to see which MSN-affiliated stores currently are providing free shipping and view a calendar of shops that will offer free shipping in the coming weeks.

Like Yahoo! Shopping, MSN eShop offers express checkout services. MSN shoppers can set up a Passport wallet, which stores your name, credit card information, and shipping address. On your next visit to an MSN eShop, you can use your Passport wallet, rather than having to stop and fill out each individual store's credit and shipping forms.

Finally, remember that eShop is just one of the services offered through MSN. If you click on the **Home** button in the menu bar, which can be found across the top of every Web page, you'll link to MSN's home page.

The eShop Auction home page contains links to information that explains how the site works and how visitors can sign up to start bidding and selling.

Consumer Guide Network

www.cgnetwork.com

If you've ever shopped for a vehicle, chances are you've used a Consumer Guide publication while doing your research. Now you can access this popular car guide, as well as other Consumer Guide publications, via the Web.

Consumer Guide's home page contains links to car guides, best buy information on a wide range of products, recipe and cooking guides, and an online bookstore. Those who are unfamiliar with the publishing company's reputation may want to click on the **About Consumer Guide** link, which is located on the home page. You'll find a short history of the company, learn how it rates the vehicles it reviews, and discover what criteria is used to determine which items will be deemed "best buys."

The **Auto Guide** at this site is awesome. You can read reviews and search for a new car yourself, or you can use the **Personal Shopper**. This service is free if you register with the site, and it offers a no-hassle, no-pressure approach to purchasing a new car.

Select the make and model of the vehicle you're looking for, enter how you can be reached, and within 24 hours a Personal Shopper will contact you with a competitive, prearranged price, financing options, and the vehicle's location.

You also can apply to lease a car online, get help with financing, and calculate your monthly car payment. If you're considering a lease, take a moment to read about the two types of leasing options dealers offer.

The most helpful link, however, is the one that gives buying advice. You can find out which new cars are best for you by using an interactive car finder, shop for a car loan, get some sound negotiating tips, and find out what rights you have as a consumer following the purchase of a new car.

Used car shoppers also can find plenty of useful information. You can get shopping tips, access repair and recall reports, obtain pricing information, get an instant quote on some car insurance, and more.

If all this car shopping has made you hungry, click on the **Recipes** link located in the main menu bar at the top of each page. You'll link to a searchable database of more than 1,000 brand-name recipes. This link also contains meal ideas and several useful cooking guides.

Consumer Guide's popular auto guides are now on the Web. New car shoppers can link to see pictures of the automobiles, read road test reports, get the auto's specifications, obtain pricing information, and much more.

PLANETRX.COM

www.planetrx.com

E-mail: customercare@planetrx.com

Many seniors spend a lot of money on over-the-counter drugs and prescription medications. PlanetRx.com, an online pharmacy and health information service, not only offers shoppers an opportunity to save money, users also can link to get more information about the diseases or conditions that affect them.

The quickest way to find out if you'll save money on over-the-counter medicines is to enter the product's name in the site's internal search engine, click the **Go** button, and start comparison shopping. To find out if you can save money on prescription medications, click on the **Pharmacy** tab, and then link to **Price Quotes**. If you see a savings, you can transfer your prescription. However, you'll have to complete the site's free registration first.

If you want to fill a new prescription, you'll need to provide PlanetRx.com with your doctor's name and information about your insurance coverage, if you have any. PlanetRx.com then will check to see if your insurer is part of their network, and they'll send you an e-mail confirmation.

Once you've completed this process, you'll be able to fill prescriptions with ease. PlanetRx.com will create an account for you and store all of your insurance information in a secure environment. When you return to the site later you won't have to enter this information again, unless you've changed insurance plans.

Keep in mind, however, that filling a prescription at an online pharmacy doesn't work the same as popping into your local drugstore. If you get a written prescription, you'll need to mail it to PlanetRx.com to be filled.

The most efficient way to get your medication is to have your doctor phone in your prescription. Or you can ask PlanetRx.com to phone the doctor for you. Your prescription will arrive via the U.S. Postal Service or by FedEx overnight or two-day delivery. (To view these rates, click on **Help** and then link to **Shipping & Handling**.)

In addition to prescription and over-the-counter drugs, PlanetRx.com sells vitamins and herbs, beauty products, personal care items, and medical supplies. Visitors also can find information about drug interactions, or visit one of PlanetRx.com's satellite Web sites, such as Arthritis.com or Diabetes.com, to learn more about a specific disease or condition.

PlanetRx.com also serves as an online community for those who want to share their concerns about a particular health condition. The site sponsors many special guest events featuring people such as Deepak Chopra, M.D., a well-known expert on alternative medicine, and Miss America 1999, Nicole Johnson, who has diabetes.

More than just an online drugstore, PlanetRx.com's Web site contains links to several satellite sites where visitors can learn more about a specific disease or condition, such as high cholesterol.

PEAPOD

www.peapod.com

E-mail: Click on About Peapod.

Peapod Inc. is one of the more popular grocery services on the Web. Despite its popularity, however, this service currently is available only in select metropolitan areas. To see if Peapod is available where you live, access the Web site and click on **Check it out**. Next, enter your ZIP code and see if the service is available in your area. If it is, you're in luck.

The quickest way to get started is to click on **Express Shop**. Next, type a short description of the items you need, such as cereal, milk, and eggs. You can specify a brand name, a manufacturer's name, or a category or type of product. For example, you can specify the brand name of cereal you want, such as Cheerios, or you can search by the manufacturer's name, General Mills.

Next, make sure you've spelled the items on your list correctly. If you're unsure of the spelling, enter only the first few letters of the word. Also, don't use plurals or apostrophes. Finally, click on **Start Shopping**. Peapod will allow you to sort items by price so you can find the best value, or you can sort by calories or other dietary criteria if nutrition is a concern. The items you select will appear in your "shopping cart" along the right side of the page. Each item you've placed in the cart is listed, along with the total amount you've spent.

Once you're done shopping, click on **Checkout**. You'll be asked to register with Peapod and choose the time you'd like to have your groceries delivered. Delivery prices vary by city, so be sure to click on **Prices & Delivery Areas** to see how much Peapod charges where you live. Overall, however, delivery charges are nominal. You might even wind up saving money, particularly if you often buy on impulse when you do your grocery shopping. In addition, coupon clippers don't have to worry about missing out on special bargains. The company's delivery drivers accept manufacturers' coupons, and the amount you save by using coupons will be credited to your account. Peapod also allows you to send back any grocery item you deem unsatisfactory for a full refund.

Peapod's online store is arranged just like a regular grocery store. This screen shows icons with the various aisles you can browse within the virtual grocery store.

BARNES & NOBLE

www.barnesandnoble.com

If you think your local Barnes & Noble store has an impressive selection, just wait until you visit their cybershop. This retail giant wants to be the #1 bookseller in cyberspace, and its offerings are impressive. Visitors can shop for books, music, magazines, prints and posters, and more.

The site contains many of the same features found at rival Amazon.com's Web site. For example, Barnes & Noble's **Pick and Click** provides visitors with one-click shopping convenience, and there's no shortage of bargain books. A number of features, however, make it stand out from the competition.

Barnes & Noble has compiled a list of links to popular book series, such as the Dummies books and the Independent Thinker series. Its internal search engine is good—allowing visitors to narrow their quest by subject, price, and format—and those looking for children's books can shop by age range. The online bookstore also features thousands of book reviews from respected sources such as *Publishers Weekly*, *Kirkus Reviews*, *The New York Times Book Review*, *Salon*, and *Library Journal*.

Barnes & Noble offers electronic gift certificates, and you can get your books gift wrapped in the paper of your choice. A selection of free, electronic greeting cards also can be found at the site.

Visitors can sign up to be notified about new book releases by e-mail, or they can attend one of the online chats hosted by Barnes & Noble that feature many well-known authors. If you choose to register with the site, you can sign up to receive one or more of the store's 60 free online newsletters, which contain reviews, recommendations, special deals, articles, and updates on new books, software, and music.

The site also allows you to find the Barnes & Noble store nearest you by typing in your ZIP code. Given the online selection and service, however, you may not ever want to go to one of their retail stores again. Still, the Barnes & Noble shopping experience just isn't the same without getting a cup of Starbucks coffee.

You don't have to give up Starbucks just because you're shopping online, however. To order some java, click on the **Buy Starbucks Coffee** link, which can be found on the home page. That way, you can brew a pot before you venture out on your next online shopping excursion.

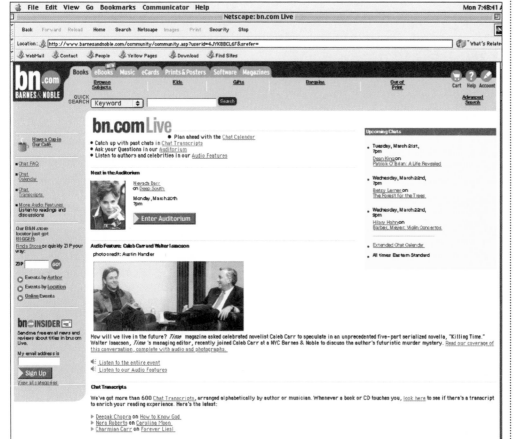

Retail bookseller Barnes & Noble also has a cyberstore that hosts many online events, including live chats with well-known authors.

Chapter 7
Health

DR. KOOP

www.drkoop.com

E-mail: feedback@drkoop.com

Dr. Koop is a must-visit Web site for those interested in getting medical information online. This award-winning site was developed by former U.S. Surgeon General C. Everett Koop, who believes the best way to keep people healthy is to empower them with knowledge.

When you first glance at this site's home page, you may feel overwhelmed. It seems like you can find information on just about everything health-related. Although it's tempting to just plunge right in and start browsing, begin by searching for the information you really need. You can always go back to the home page and start surfing when you're done.

Across the top of the home page you'll find a menu bar of hyperlinked tabs that will transport you to the main sections within the site. The **Family** tab will take you to the Family Health Center. Once you've linked to this section, click on **Aging Healthy** to get some suggestions on what you need to do in order to live well and live longer. The Family Health Center also contains sections dedicated to health problems faced by men and women. ABC medical correspondent Dr. Nancy Snyderman's daily column, which covers women's health issues such as breast exams and menopause, also can be found in this section.

The **Resources** tab contains a wealth of information and tools. You'll find links to a personal drugstore where you can fill or refill your prescriptions online; a medical encyclopedia; information about how you can volunteer to participate in a clinical drug trial; information about health insurance; and reviews about other medical sites on the Web.

If you've been trying to quit smoking or are looking for tips about fitness, click on the **Wellness** tab. You'll find advice on nutrition, fitness, and smoking cessation.

You can even access a comprehensive archive of health-related news by clicking on the **News** tab. To find information, type in a keyword and click on the **Search Now** button to access the collection of articles.

Those who suffer from a chronic illness, and those who serve as their caretakers, will find a group of like-minded souls by clicking on the **Community** tab. Here you'll find a number of interactive communities where you can communicate, through online chats and message boards, with people who share similar health experiences. To use these services, you'll need to register (for free) with the site.

Finally, for information about a specific disease, condition, or health-related topic, click on the **Conditions** tab. You'll find several different directories you can browse.

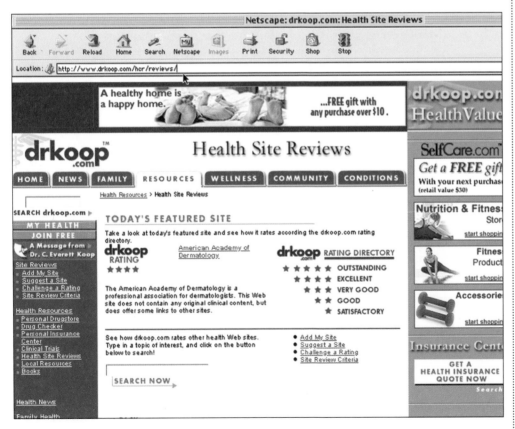

*When you're seeking medical information, your source's credibility is crucial. If you want to know how Dr. Koop rates other health-related Web sites, click on the **Resources** tab and link to **Health Site Reviews**.*

HEALTHATOZ.COM

www.healthatoz.com

E-mail: info@healthatoz.com

HealthAtoZ.com was developed by health-care professionals, and it contains resources for people of all ages. This comprehensive Web site is divided into six main sections.

Of particular interest in the **Your Family** section is the 60-something+ link. Here you'll find health resources for seniors and links such as **Cholesterol after 65: Where's the Beef?**, **Is Aging the Last Great Fallacy?**, and **Resources for Caregivers**. Other helpful links in this section include an **Osteoporosis Diary** that allows you to track your daily calcium intake and one that gives seniors tips for coping with asthma.

In the **Condition Forums** section, you can find news and information about diseases and conditions that affect you or your loved ones. You also can share your experiences and health concerns with others by linking to one of the section's message boards.

The **Wellness Center** link will transport you to one of the Internet's first virtual fitness centers. You can take a fitness quiz here or ask the fitness center's personal trainer a question. Be sure to check out the **Senior Fit** link, which contains information on the health benefits of weight training, walking, tai chi, and more. You also might want to view the ever-growing list of fitness resources available for seniors before leaving this section of the site.

Back on the home page you'll find links to many health-related news stories as well as some **Cool Tools**, such as the one that allows you to calculate your target heart rate. A database of health topics, which are listed in alphabetical order (hence, the site's name), also can be found on the home page.

Before leaving HealthAtoZ.com's Web site, be sure to check out **E-Mate**. This feature allows you to organize all of your family's medical information, and it is free to those who register with the site. You can schedule e-mail reminders of important health events, track your diet, maintain your health records, store the addresses and phone numbers of your family's doctors, and find out how your lifestyle and habits can potentially affect your health and longevity. Finally, if you're concerned about disclosing all this personal information, you can put your mind at ease by reading the site's privacy statement.

HealthAtoZ.com contains a list of conditions and diseases that you can browse. For example, the page on macular degeneration contains information on this condition, a risk-assessment quiz, self-management tools, and a link to a message board where you can post your thoughts.

MENTAL HEALTH NET

http://mentalhelp.net

E-mail: webmaster@cmhc.com

First thing's first. Let's make sure you're at the right Web site. You should be at Mental Health Net (MHN). If you're somewhere else, check the Web address and make sure you've typed in "mentalhelp" and not "mentalhealth."

MHN is run by psychologist Mark Dombeck, Ph.D., and is sponsored by CMHC, a mental health-software development company. Launched in 1995, this award-winning site has a variety of different resources for those interested in mental health, psychology, and psychiatry.

The site is divided into three main sections: **Disorders & Treatments**, **Professional Resources**, and **MHN's Reading Room**. The **Disorders & Treatments** section contains links to information about many common psychological disorders. You also can find links to various support resources here.

Speaking of support resources, MHN's online community hosts a number of online support groups and chat rooms that allow registered members to interact with other members who are dealing with mental health issues. You can also find forums on depression, anxiety, bipolar disorder, relationships, and more.

Also worth checking out in this section are two links to great books. The first book, *Psychological Self-Help*, reviews all aspects of self-improvement; the second book, *Self-Help Source Book Online*, helps readers find support organizations for medical and mental illness-related problems.

Unless you have worked in the health-care field, you'll probably want to skip over the **Professional Resources** section and move right on to **MHN's Reading Room**. This is the place to get the answers to the questions you've always wanted to ask.

In **The Experts Corner**, you'll find links that allow you to get relationship advice or ask a pharmacist a question. You also can link to ask the MHN director a question concerning mental illness, mental health, psychotherapy, and other related topics. In addition, you can link to MHN's monthly commentary, participate in an online poll, or click to read *Perspectives*, MHN's electronic magazine.

A number of current news items can be found on the home page as well. While on the home page, be sure to click on the **Lighten Up** icon to read some mental health and psychology jokes, which are actually quite tasteful.

Before leaving this site, click on the **Bookstore** icon. You will be linked to in-depth book reviews written by MHN's contributors, who hail from many various backgrounds and perspectives.

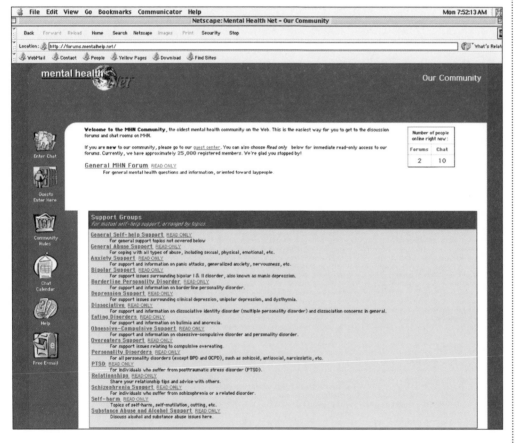

This screen shows some of the many self-help forums sponsored by Mental Health Net (MHN). To use this service, you must register with MHN. Registration is free and confidential.

ASK DR. WEIL

www.drweil.com

E-mail: drweil@thehealthpages.com

Ask Dr. Weil is a must-visit Web site if you take vitamins, think there's something to this business about herbs and healing, and are frustrated with conventional medicine. In case you don't know who Dr. Weil is, here's the scoop.

Dr. Weil, a graduate of Harvard Medical School, specializes in alternative medicine, mind-body interactions, and medical botany. He's also the author of seven books about such topics. At his Web site, you can link to ask the good doctor a question or review earlier queries in the **Q&A Library**. From the **Health Pages** section, you can link to a department devoted to seniors' health needs.

You'll find links to articles on everything from how to cover the gaps in Medicare to how to choose a nursing home. In the **Self-Help** section, you'll find a database that allows you to search for a holistic healer in your area. Another link allows you to sign up for Dr. Weil's online 8 Weeks to Optimum Health program. Based on his book *8 Weeks to Optimum Health*, the program apparently has quite a following, as evidenced by the number of messages posted about the program on the site's online bulletin board.

You also can link to Dr. Ruth Westheimer's site. Here, visitors can ask America's foremost sex therapist questions or read her advice column. Another interesting link at the site is the Healing Center with Bernie Siegel, M.D. Dr. Siegel founded Exceptional Cancer Patients (ECaP), a style of individual and group therapy based on "carefrontation," a loving, safe, therapeutic confrontation enabling everyone to understand his or her healing potential. He also has written about the mind-body connection in medicine, and his columns encourage patients to take an active role in the healing process. This section also contains links to support groups for people whose lives are affected by a serious illness.

Before moving on to another Web site, consider signing up for one of the free weekly newsletters authored by Dr. Weil, Dr. Ruth, or Dr. Siegel. Dr. Weil also offers to send visitors a free trial issue of his popular *Self Healing* newsletter so they can see if it's right for them.

THE HEALTH NETWORK

www.thehealthnetwork.com

E-mail: webmaster@thehealthnetwork.com

The Health Network was formed through an equal partnership between FOX Entertainment Group and AHN Partners, L.P. What does that mean? It means you'll find an interesting mix of entertainment and information at this Web site.

That's not a bad thing, however. In fact, The Health Network has become one of the most-visited health-information sites on the Web thanks to some live medical events that it broadcast. The Health Network reaches more than 17 million households in all 50 states through cable and satellite and millions more via the Internet.

This site contains a lot of good resources. You can learn about upcoming health programs, get the latest news, and find easy-to-understand, in-depth health information. You also can chat with credible medical professionals and with other folks who are interested in a specific health condition, such as arthritis.

The site is divided into three main sections: **Medical**, **Communities**, and **Departments**. The **Medical** section lists and describes common diseases and conditions. Of particular interest are the links to **Arthritis**, **Osteoarthritis**, **Osteoporosis**, and **Prostate Cancer**. Within each of these topics you can find links to informative articles, books about the chosen subject, and other Web resources.

The **Communities** section contains health advocacy tips and links to consumer topics, such as managed health care and long-term health care. You also can link to view a list of the nation's top 100 orthopedic hospitals as rated by HCIA Inc., which collects, manages, and distributes comparative health-care information.

The **Departments** section contains a **Community Profiler**, which allows you to view the rates of certain health-related behaviors and conditions in your community. You can see the rates for health indicators like average height and weight, cigarette smoking, alcohol consumption, visits to doctors, income, and more. This section also contains a link to **LifeMasters Online** health-management program, which stresses self-care, education, monitoring, and support for those with chronic health conditions.

Back on the home page, you can find links to informative news articles or click to view The Health Network's TV listing of upcoming programs. You also can link to an online health chat or view a list of upcoming community events.

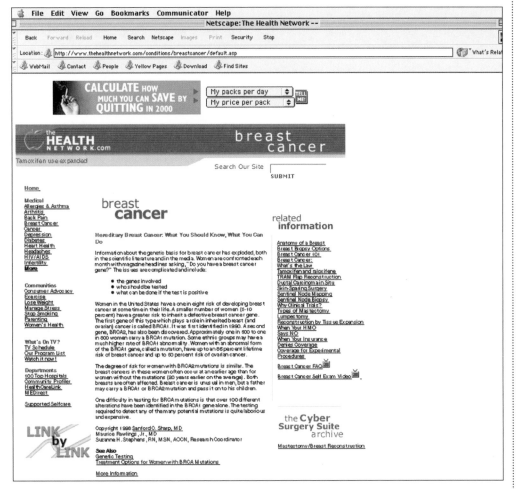

The Health Network contains a wealth of resources, including an excellent section on breast cancer. This section contains links to information closely associated with breast cancer as well.

ALLHEALTH.COM

www.allhealth.com

E-mail: support@allhealth.com

The Women's Network hosts allHealth.com. However, this well-rounded Web site contains resources everyone will find useful. One of the more striking features about iVillage's allHealth.com is its personal touch. If you can't find an answer to a question, you can send an e-mail to support@allhealth.com, or you can link to **Ask Caro** for a more personal response.

At allHealth.com, you can search for health information by category, read the latest health news, or post a message on one of the site's many online bulletin boards. You also can participate in one of the site's scheduled online health and fitness chats.

This site's search engine gives visitors several query options. You can choose to search allHealth.com, iVillage.com, or use Snap.com to scour the Web. In addition, allHealth.com has two comprehensive drug databases. Visitors can search by drug name or browse an alphabetical list of commonly prescribed drugs. A number of other helpful links cover questions about over-the-counter drugs and medication problems. You also can link to read more about Evista, a new drug being prescribed for postmenopausal women at risk for developing osteoporosis.

Although you will find a lot of medical information aimed at women, the **Main Centers** section of this site includes links to **Men's Health**, **Alternative Health**, and **Senior Health**. The **Senior Health** section contains articles of interest to seniors and their caregivers, and you can find a number of links to age-specific health problems.

Other interesting sections at allHealth.com's Web site include a searchable database of eldercare services and a link to the **Online Psych Center**. Here you'll find an IQ test, an emotional intelligence test, several personality tests, a number of relationship quizzes, and more.

In the **Special Centers** section you can get information on specific conditions and diseases—such as asthma, breast care, and fitness—or link to read *Heart Watch*, a newsletter published by the *New England Journal of Medicine*. You also can sign up to receive a number of free online newsletters published by iVillage about subjects ranging from men's health to pain management.

If you still have a question after browsing the site, you can link to the **Ask an Expert** section. Here you'll find the questions and answers to many common ailments, or you can link to contact a health-care expert via e-mail.

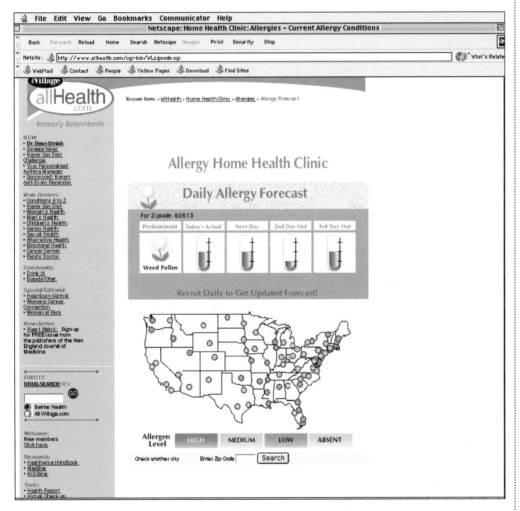

Got the sniffles? Enter your zip code into allHealth.com's Pollen Count database to find out what allergens are prevalent in your area of the country.

AMERICAN DIABETES ASSOCIATION

www.diabetes.org

E-mail: customerservice@diabetes.org

Of the many condition-specific medical sites that can be found on the Web, the American Diabetes Association (ADA) site stands out as one of the best. A nonprofit organization, the ADA's Web site is well-organized, easy to use, and contains an excellent reference area.

Visitors can find information about diabetes research, read news articles and press releases, and link to *Diabetes Forecast*, the association's health and wellness magazine. Those with backgrounds in health care also will appreciate the links to several resources aimed at professionals.

If you or a loved one were recently diagnosed with diabetes, this site is an excellent place to obtain information. Click on the **Newly Diagnosed** link to get general information and learn about new medical treatments. According to the ADA, diabetes is more common among African Americans, Hispanics, Native Americans, Asian Americans, and Pacific Islanders. With this in mind, the ADA has developed information and programs that target these groups. For example, Hispanics can find information written in Spanish, and African Americans can link to the ADA's **African American Program**, which contains some really good information about how to live with this disease.

Indeed, the toughest part of having a chronic disease is learning how to deal with it for the long haul. The ADA recognizes this, and you can find plenty of links that offer both encouragement and good, hard facts.

Speaking of good, hard facts, check out the **Shop Our Store** section of the site. You'll find a number of recommended books written for consumers, some cookbooks for people with diabetes, and a number of publications geared toward health-care professionals.

The **Advocacy/Legal Issues** section of the ADA's Web site also is well done. You'll find links to information about what's being done to find a cure for the disease, efforts to improve health-care coverage, and efforts to stop discrimination in the school and the workplace.

Although the ADA's site is excellent, remember that it's not the only site of its genre on the Web. When you get a moment, flip back to the Appendix and look under the Health heading to find a list of additional Web sites that contain information and resources about other diseases or health conditions.

File   Edit   View   Go   Bookmarks   Communicator   Help

Netscape:

Back   Forward   Reload   Home   Search   Netscape   Images   Print   Security   Stop

Location: http://www.diabetes.org/ada/risktest.asp   What's Relat

WebMail   Contact   People   Yellow Pages   Download   Find Sites

Learn About ADA
About ADA
Career Opportunities
Annual Report
About Our Corporate
Sponsors
Disclaimer

Donate Now
How and Why to Donate
Memorial Contributions
Establish a Planned Gift
The Elizabeth Knight Fund

Diabetes Info
General Information
In the News
Newly Diagnosed
Nutrition
Exercise
Take the Risk Test
Tip of the Day
Recipe of the Day
Clinical Practice
Recommendations
African American Program

**Become a Member /
Subscribe**
Professional Membership
General Membership

Shop Our Store
Bookstore Main Page
Consumer Books
Cookbooks
Professional Books

**Magazines / Journals
Consumer Magazines**
Diabetes Forecast
Professional Journals
Clinical Diabetes
Diabetes
Diabetes Care
Diabetes Reviews
Diabetes Spectrum

For Professionals
Clinical Practice
Recommendations
Councils
Journals
Membership
Recognition
Research
Professional Education

Recognized Providers
Physicians
Education Programs

Diabetes Risk Test
Copyright © 2000 American Diabetes Association
If your browser does not support forms, try our text-only version.

Could you have diabetes and not know it?

Sixteen million Americans have diabetes - one in three does not know it! Take this test to
see if you are at risk for having diabetes. Diabetes is more common in African Americans,
Hispanics/Latinos, American Indians, Asian-Americans and Pacific Islanders. If you are a
member of one of these ethnic groups, you need to pay special attention to this test. To find
out if you are at risk answer the following questions and click on "CALCULATE" to see what
information is returned.

Please select your age category.
○ 0-45
○ 46-64
○ 65 or Older

Please select your height.
[3' ▼] [0" ▼]

Please enter your weight in pounds.
[_____]

**I am a woman who has had a baby weighing more than nine pounds at
birth.**
○ True
◉ False

I have a sister or brother with diabetes.
○ True
◉ False

I have a parent with diabetes.
○ True
◉ False

I get little or no exercise during a normal day.
○ True
◉ False

[CALCULATE] your score or [Reset] this form.

According to the ADA, of the 16 million Americans with diabetes, one in three don't know they have it. This screen shows an online test developed by the ADA that can help you determine if you're at risk for developing this disease.

New York Online Access to Health

www.noah.cuny.edu

E-mail: webmaster@noah.cuny.edu

Don't let this site's name fool you. The New York Online Access to Health (NOAH) Web site originally was started to help the citizens of New York, but this award-winning online health resource now is federally funded.

The materials at this site are up to date and very reliable. A board of doctors and other medical professionals oversee NOAH, and you'll find information here in both English and Spanish.

When you first visit this Web site, click on **Health Topics** and then link to **Aging and Alzheimer's Disease**. This link contains a list of many common health problems faced by seniors, such as cataracts and vision problems, osteoporosis, and prostate problems. You also can get the latest news about what's being done in the field of geriatric research and link to several good resources that cover the care and treatment of older adults.

Other links of interest in the **Health Topics** section include **Arthritis**, **Cancer**, **Diabetes**, **Personal Health**, and **Heart Disease & Stroke**. If you click on **Heart Disease & Stroke**, you'll find information about the best hospitals for treating heart attacks and strokes, as rated by *U.S. News & World Report*.

To help make navigating this site a little easier, NOAH gives you the option of browsing an alphabetical index of health topics. You also can use the site's internal search engine, which is powered by Excite, to search by keyword or concept. Finally, to get a better idea of how the site is organized, click on the **Help** link.

Most of the links at NOAH will transport you to state and federal health resources. In fact, if you're researching a particular health condition, this site is a great place to begin. NOAH already has scoured and compiled a set of links to some of the better health resources on the Web. Like many good Web sites, NOAH also includes a **What's New** page. Given the number of links on this page, it's clear that NOAH is committed to providing consumers with the most up-to-date health-care information.

Finally, if you live in New York, take a little time to see what health resources are available in your state. You also might find the link to New York Public Library helpful.

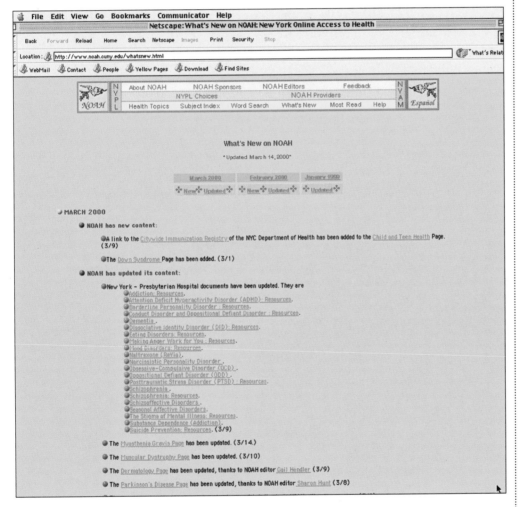

*NOAH's **What's New** page lists information at the site that has been added or revised within the past three months. To view this page in Spanish, click on the **Español** icon, which is located on the right side of the menu bar.*

MAYO CLINIC HEALTH OASIS

www.mayohealth.org

E-mail: oasis@mayo.edu

Mayo Clinic Health Oasis promises to give visitors "Reliable Information for a Healthier Life." This Web site—which is an extension of Mayo Clinic and is directed by a team of Mayo physicians, scientists, writers, and educators—is updated daily. An editorial board at Mayo Clinic identifies the health topics and selects specialists as expert sources for each article found on the site.

The information you'll find on this site is reliable. Every article includes the date on which it is placed on the site. In addition, any article more than three years old is reviewed to make sure it is still accurate.

Through this Web site, visitors have access to the experience and knowledge of the more than 1,200 physicians and scientists at Mayo Clinic. In fact, one of the more interesting links allows visitors to **Ask Mayo**. The **Ask Mayo** link lets you ask a Mayo Clinic physician a question about a disease or condition or ask a Mayo Clinic dietitian a question about diet and nutrition.

All of the health information at this site is written in easy-to-understand language. The **Library** link contains a wide range of information about maintaining your health and treating specific diseases and conditions, and you can access a database of explanations of how to treat common and uncommon illnesses.

You also can find practical first-aid advice for hundreds of different accidents and ailments and test your health and nutrition knowledge. Those on a restricted diet can link to a virtual cookbook that contains a variety of healthy recipes. A dietitian also gives tips on how to cut fat, calories, cholesterol, or salt from your diet without cutting back on taste.

The online glossary of definitions and medical terms at this site is excellent. You can read a definition and hear a word's pronunciation by clicking on the term. The site's internal search engine provides several options for finding information, and you can even subscribe to a weekly e-mail update published by Mayo Clinic Health Oasis.

Visitors will appreciate the fact that the Web site's staff has taken the time to research and include links to a number of other health-oriented sites on the Web that contain valuable information. This site's commitment to excellence is

admirable, and the advertisements on the site are clearly labeled so you can distinguish them from the editorial content. Like Dr. Koop and HealthAtoZ.com, Mayo Clinic Health Oasis also conforms to the HON (Health on the Net Foundation) code of ethics for health-care sites.

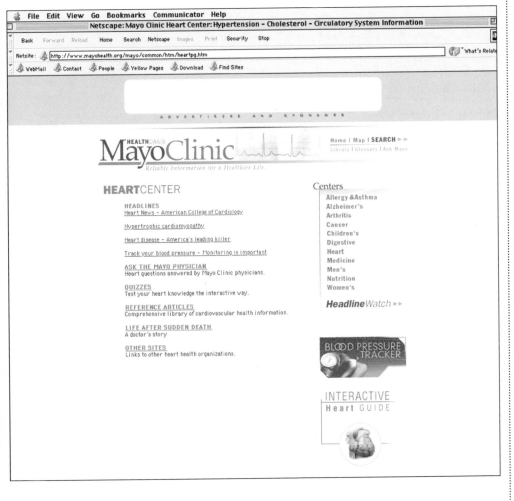

*Mayo Clinic Health Oasis contains links to several centers of information, such as the **Heart Center**, where visitors can find news and quizzes and even link to an interactive guide.*

Chapter 8
Travel

PRICELINE.COM
www.priceline.com

E-mail: Click on the E-mail us link.

Priceline.com is a popular Web site among leisure travelers. This travel site allows you to name the price you're willing to pay for an airline ticket or hotel room. Here's how it works.

On Priceline.com's home page you'll see an **Airline Ticket** search engine. Enter your departure city and state, arrival city and state/country, and the number of tickets you need. Then click on the **Next** button to submit your information.

Next you'll be asked to fill in the dates you'd like to travel, the airports from which you are willing to depart, the airports at which you are willing to arrive, and other information, such as whether you are willing to fly on a non-jet aircraft. Finally you'll be asked to fill in the amount you are willing to pay for each round-trip plane ticket.

If you're not sure what price to name, research the lowest published airfare available for your travel dates. To do this, you might want to do a little checking around at Microsoft Expedia, *msn.expedia.com*, or Preview Travel, *www.previewtravel.com*. If you don't want to take time to check either of these online travel reservation systems, just enter the highest amount you're willing to pay. You can name any price you want, but the more reasonable your price, the greater the chances that it will be accepted by an airline. If you're strapped for cash or are just looking to cut costs, check out the list of sponsors that will help pay for your ticket. For example, if you agree to switch your phone service to Sprint, another $40 will be added to your offer for free.

If the price you name is unrealistic, Priceline.com will let you know that. A screen will appear that will give you the opportunity to select additional departure and arrival airports. Priceline.com also will suggest the amount to which you should increase your bid. However, you can choose to raise the bid by any

amount you wish, keep your existing bid, or ask for more information about a sponsor who will help pay for your ticket.

Next, review all the information you've submitted thus far. You'll also be given the opportunity to review Priceline.com's terms and conditions and indicate your acceptance of these terms. Once that's out of the way, you'll be prompted to fill out an online form with your name, billing address, daytime and evening phone numbers, credit card number, and e-mail address. This page is secure, as indicated by the Web address that begins with "https" and the padlock that appears in the lower left corner of your screen (if you are using Microsoft Internet Explorer). You also can link to read about the security measures used to encrypt your personal information so it can't be accessed by computer hackers.

Once you click on **Submit My Request**, Priceline.com will look for major airlines that are willing to accept your offer. You'll be notified by e-mail in an hour or less. If an airline accepts your offer, Priceline.com will lock in the price

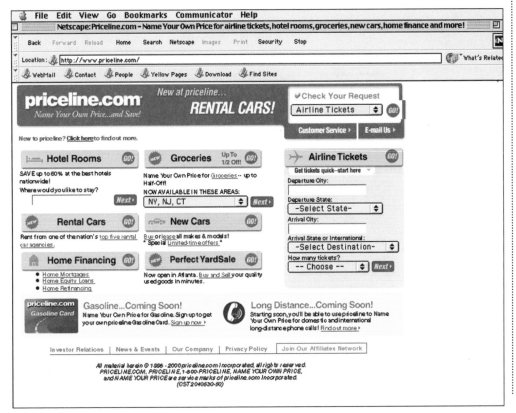

*Priceline.com's home page contains an online form that allows visitors to search for low-price airline tickets. Enter your departure city and state, arrival city and state/country, and the number of tickets you need, and click on **Next** to begin your search.*

and purchase your tickets automatically using the credit card information you provided. You'll get charged only the price you named, plus any applicable taxes and fees.

If your price isn't accepted by an airline, your credit card won't be charged. You then can submit a new request by making a few changes.

To save even more money on airline tickets, you can select a sponsor who will add anywhere from $10 to $60 to the amount of your offer. For example, if you apply for a Discover card, the company will apply $60 toward the cost of your ticket.

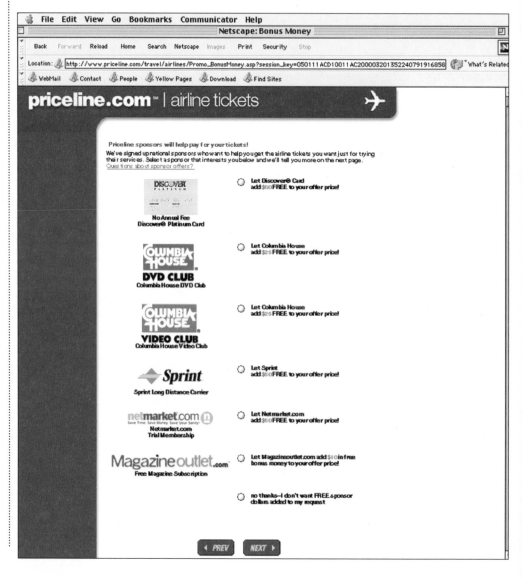

File   Edit   View   Go   Bookmarks   Communicator   Help

Netscape: Increase your Chances!

Back   Forward   Reload   Home   Search   Netscape   Images   Print   Security   Stop

Location: http://www.priceline.com/travel/airlines/MaxChances.asp?session_key=050111ACD10011AC200003201352240791916858800   What's Related

WebMail   Contact   People   Yellow Pages   Download   Find Sites

priceline.com℠ | airline tickets ✈

We really want you to get your airline tickets!

Based on past priceline customer ticket requests *for the cities and dates that you have chosen*, an offer price of $150 per ticket has a very low chance of getting accepted by a major airline.

We would be happy to submit any request you like, but if you really want your airline tickets to SAN FRANCISCO, CALIFORNIA we strongly recommend that you:

▶ Select an additional departure airport
Certain airlines only fly out of specific airports. If you agree to depart from additional airports, more airlines will consider your offer price.

- ☑ CHICAGO – OHARE INTL, IL (ORD)
- ☐ CHICAGO – MEIGS FIELD, IL (CGX)
- ☐ CHICAGO – MIDWAY, IL (MDW)

▶ Select an additional arrival airport
Certain airlines only fly out of specific airports. If you agree to arrive at additional airports, more airlines will consider your offer price.

- ☑ SAN FRANCISCO INTL, CA (SFO)
- ☐ SAN JOSE INTL, CA (SJC)
- ☐ OAKLAND INTL, CA (OAK)

▶ Increase your offer price by $75 or more
Most airlines will consider your offer if you can raise your price.

- ○ I want to raise my offer price to $ [   ] .00 per ticket
- ○ Tell me about sponsors who will help me pay for my tickets
- ○ I want to keep my price at $150 per ticket

◀ PREV   NEXT ▶

priceline.com home | customer service | e-mail us | about priceline.com | privacy policy

All material herein © 2000 priceline.com Incorporated, all rights reserved
PRICELINE.COM, PRICELINE, 1-800-PRICELINE, NAME YOUR OWN PRICE,
and NAME YOUR PRICE are service marks of priceline.com Incorporated.
(CST 2040530-50)

ws-69

If you enter an unrealistic bid, Priceline.com will encourage you to increase the dollar amount or add additional departure and arrival airports, which may influence the ticket's price. You also can choose to hear more about a sponsor that can help pay for your ticket.

PREVIEW TRAVEL

www.previewtravel.com

E-mail: feedback@previewtravel.com

Do-it-yourselfers will enjoy Preview Travel's Web site. This site contains everything you need to research and book your own trip. At first glance, Preview Travel's home page contains an overwhelming number of links. Not only will you find several online reservation systems, but you also can link to check the weather at your intended destination, see what the current currency conversion rate is, get travel tips and advice, or visit a video or photo gallery to view places you might like to visit.

To get the most out of this site, you'll need to register with Preview Travel. Registration is free. When registering, you'll be given the option of creating and storing a travel profile, complete with frequent-flyer numbers. If you plan on visiting this site frequently, it's probably worth the time and effort to create your own travel profile. Before doing this, however, you might want to click on the **Preview Travel Guarantee** link, which can be found at the top of the registration page, so you can get the details about this site's privacy policy.

After registering with the site, print out your Account Confirmation and store it in a safe place. That way, you can easily access this information if you should forget your member name or password at a future time. Once that task is out of the way, you're ready to begin your travel planning. Preview Travel's planning services allow you to make air, hotel, and rental car reservations. You also can create and save travel itineraries or register for airfare alerts, which will come to you via e-mail and notify you about discounted flights.

Making air, hotel, or rental car reservations is simple because Preview Travel walks visitors through the entire process. You'll also be able to view and change many travel options, such as the flight option; the changes can affect the price of your trip. When you're ready, you can simply book your reservations online.

Although Preview Travel has its own Web site, America Online (AOL) members can access this company by using the keywords Preview Travel. Preview Travel is an AOL Certified Merchant, which means the company meets or exceeds AOL's service standards.

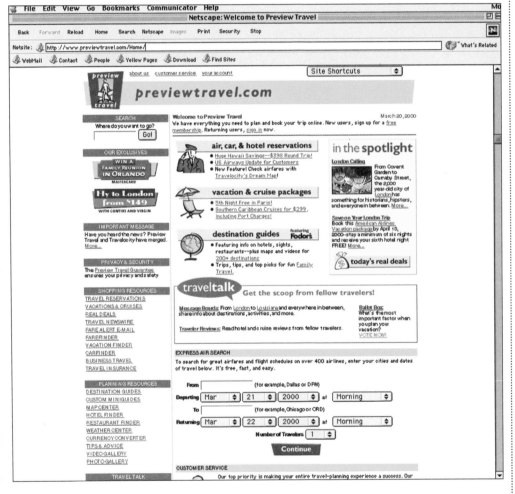

Preview Travel's home page contains links to online air, car, and hotel reservation systems; travel guides; vacation and cruise packages; and airfare specials.

EXPEDIA

http://msn.expedia.com

E-mail: travel@expedia.com

It's easy to see why Expedia Inc. has won so many awards. This Web site, which is part of the Microsoft Network, contains every resource imaginable for travelers. Expedia gives visitors access to more than 450 airlines, 40,000 hotels, and every major car rental agency. You also can find more than 400 destination guides at this site.

Like Preview Travel, Expedia has many features that allow registered members to customize their experience. In the **My Travel** section of the home page, you'll find a link that allows registered users to store trip information so they can review it later. You also can create your own personal profile, which includes your airline, car, and hotel preferences; track all the miles in your various frequent flyer accounts using Expedia's MileageMiner; or sign up to receive a weekly e-mail update of airfares to your favorite cities.

Cost-conscious travelers will find plenty of deals at this site. Click on **Special Deals**, and you'll link to a list of bargain-busters. You can find cruise deals, European vacations, and a host of discounted travel packages in this section.

Expedia also has a Flight Price Matcher. Enter your destination, travel dates, name, and credit card number, and tell the Flight Price Matcher how much you're willing to pay. The Flight Price Matcher will search for a flight, and you'll be notified on-screen within an hour if a match for your request is found.

If a match is found, your credit card will be charged and the flight will be booked automatically. Bear in mind that the Flight Price Matcher automatically books round-trip, coach-class tickets that are noncancelable and nonrefundable. Also, you can make only one request for each date/destination combination every seven days. (If you want to make more than one request within a seven-day period, check out Priceline.com, *www.priceline.com*.)

If the Flight Price Matcher doesn't give you the results you were hoping for, try using Expedia's Flight Wizard. The Flight Wizard is very popular among leisure travelers because it allows you to build your own flight schedule, whether it's one-way or round-trip. The Flight Wizard also allows you to check for the lowest published airfares between any two cities and search for flights at multiple airports in a single city, eliminating the need to conduct multiple searches.

In addition to helping you find airfares, rental cars, and hotel rooms, Expedia contains a number of links to vacation packages, cruises, resorts, and more. If you're shopping for a hotel or rental car, be sure to check to see if you're eligible to receive a discounted rate through AARP or AAA.

Expedia also has a Fare Compare feature. Fare Compare allows you to save time by seeing the best prices that other customers have found when using Expedia. For example, the lowest fare an Expedia member found for taking a flight between Sarasota, Florida, and Los Angeles, California, was $211.

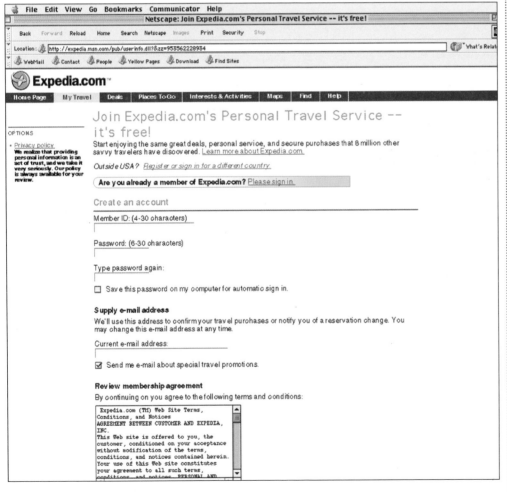

Expedia allows you to create a personal profile where you can store airline, car, and hotel preferences. You also can store your passport information in your personal profile for future reference.

Like many other travel sites, Expedia uses Secure Sockets Layer (SSL), the industry's standard security technology, to encrypt customers' data as it travels across the Internet. If you should have a problem or question, you also have the option of calling Expedia's toll-free phone number, which is posted in the **Customer Support** section.

Expedia also has a ticket-in-hand policy that takes care of customers if a ticket gets lost. Expedia handles the airline's lost-ticket fee, and the customer gets a new ticket.

Click on Expedia's **Special Deals** *link to view some discounted travel, airfare, hotel, and car rentals. You can sort these deals by destination, date, or price by clicking on a column title.*

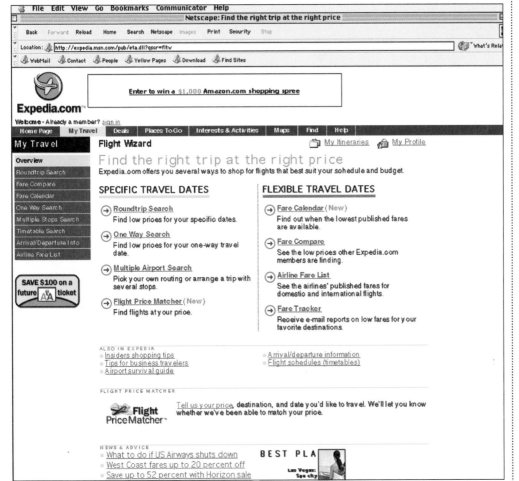

Expedia's Flight Wizard allows you to search for the lowest fares and plan your trip step by step.

GRAND CIRCLE TRAVEL

www.gct.com

E-mail: postmaster@gct.com

Grand Circle Travel promises to offer "unique experiences for seasoned travelers." The company was founded in 1958 to serve the travel needs of AARP members. Although Grand Circle Travel is no longer affiliated with AARP, it still serves more than 50,000 senior travelers each year.

Grand Circle Travel's Web site is divided into three sections. In the **Learn About Grand Circle Travel** section, visitors can link to learn more about the company or read the company's newsletter, *The Grand Circle Traveler.* The **Value**, **Pacing**, **Choice**, **Discovery** link explains the principles behind each travel program. And the **What, Where, When, and How?** link contains questions and answers about how Grand Circle Travel works.

If you want to get specific information, however, you'll need to click on the **About Grand Circle Travel** link. Here you'll find a description of the various programs for seniors offered by the company, such as all-inclusive extended vacations, escorted programs, cruises, or cruise tours. Each of these programs offers flexible pacing and special activities designed just for seniors.

The **Your Vacation Guide** section contains links to help seniors plan their trip. You can link to use the **Vacation Chooser**, which can help you plan your trip based on the region, length of stay, or type of vacation you're seeking. You also can link to view the most popular vacation packages offered through Grand Circle Travel. Visitors short on time can browse for a vacation by using the **Select a Destination** pull-down menu, which can be found in the main menu bar of each Web page at the site.

Many of the Web pages at this site also contain a **Tips** icon. Clicking on this icon will generate different travel tips. For example, Tip #18 advises you to leave all U.S. store credit cards at home when traveling. However, you should take a few major credit cards with you, such as a Visa or MasterCard. These major cards offer a better exchange rate, the protection of a charge-back provision, and quite often an extra guarantee on your purchase.

The third section, **Get More Information**, links you to an online form for requesting a free company catalog. You'll also find the company's mailing address and toll-free phone number, should you need to contact them.

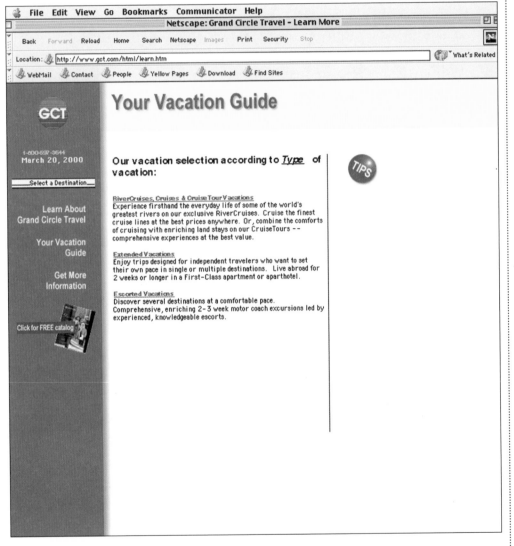

File   Edit   View   Go   Bookmarks   Communicator   Help

Netscape: Grand Circle Travel – Learn More

Back   Forward   Reload   Home   Search   Netscape   Images   Print   Security   Stop

Location: http://www.gct.com/html/learn.htm   What's Related

WebMail   Contact   People   Yellow Pages   Download   Find Sites

GCT

1-800-597-3644
March 20, 2000

Select a Destination

Learn About
Grand Circle Travel

Your Vacation
Guide

Get More
Information

Click for FREE catalog

Your Vacation Guide

Our vacation selection according to *Type* of vacation:

RiverCruises, Cruises & CruiseTourVacations
Experience firsthand the everyday life of some of the world's greatest rivers on our exclusive RiverCruises. Cruise the finest cruise lines at the best prices anywhere. Or, combine the comforts of cruising with enriching land stays on our CruiseTours -- comprehensive experiences at the best value.

Extended Vacations
Enjoy trips designed for independent travelers who want to set their own pace in single or multiple destinations. Live abroad for 2 weeks or longer in a First-Class apartment or aparthotel.

Escorted Vacations
Discover several destinations at a comfortable pace. Comprehensive, enriching 2-3 week motor coach excursions led by experienced, knowledgeable escorts.

TIPS

Grand Circle Travel offers a variety of different travel plans geared toward seniors. This screen contains links to river cruises, ocean cruises, and cruise tour vacations; extended vacations; and escorted vacations.

ELDERHOSTEL

www.elderhostel.org

E-mail: registration@elderhostel.org

If you're looking for a different kind of vacation, one that will stimulate your mind and allow you to learn and share with your peers, check out Elderhostel Inc.'s Web site. This well-respected, nonprofit organization provides many high-quality, affordable, educational adventures for adults who are 55 and older.

Founded in 1975, Elderhostel's programs were originally based on a few college campuses in New England. Today, Elderhostel serves hundreds of thousands of older adults each year who travel to residential educational programs throughout the United States and around the world.

If you're intrigued, go to the site and click on **About Our Website**. Then link to **First-Time Visitors**. This section will give you an overview of what Elderhostel has to offer. While many of the programs are educational, you also can find some that are geared toward travelers who are interested in really learning about the area they're visiting. These programs, which are held year round, usually run five to six days and often include classes, social activities, and plenty of time to just relax and enjoy. In this section you'll also find a description of the services Elderhostel provides single travelers who are 55 or older. You can even read what other singles have to say about the program.

Next, link to the **Frequently Asked Questions** to get a more in-depth look at how the various travel programs work and how much they cost. If you have a physical disability or special dietary need, don't worry. Elderhostel's programs will work with you so you'll have everything you need to enjoy your stay.

Click on the **Free Catalogs** link to get a catalog of Elderhostel's programs. You can choose to have the catalog mailed to your home, or you can register with Elderhostel and have them contact you with catalog announcements and program news via e-mail. In the meantime, click on the **Search Catalogs** link to see what's available. You can browse catalogs by state or province, or select a catalog based on the season, and then search it by topic of interest.

Given the amount of services that members of the site can access, you'll probably want to register with Elderhostel. Click on **Registration Info** to access an online registration form and learn other details, such as the deadlines and fees for each program.

File Edit View Go Bookmarks Communicator Help | Mon 8:33

Netscape: Elderhostel Adventures Afloat Catalog 99 Introduction

Back | Forward | Reload | Home | Search | Netscape | Images | Print | Security | Stop

Location: http://www.elderhostel.org/PROGOPT/Adventures.Afloat/catalog99/introduction.html | What's Relat

WebMail | Contact | People | Yellow Pages | Download | Find Sites

Main
Search the Catalogs
View Your Account
Registration Info
Elderhostel FAQ
Free Catalogs!
Contact Us
News Media
About Our Website
Get Involved

Elderhostel Adventures Afloat Catalog 2000
Welcome to Adventures Afloat

Dear Elderhostel Enthusiast,

We are pleased to offer you a variety of exciting and educational Elderhostel Adventures Afloat programs, exploring some of the world's most spectacular waterways. From the mighty and legendary Mississippi River to the deep fjords of Scandinavia, to the azure waters of the Aegean Sea, to China's most famous water route, the Yangtze River—you have a wide selection of choices in North America and around the globe.

Combining our high-quality educational programming with the invigorating experience of a shipboard excursion, Elderhostel Adventures Afloat programs provide more than just an exploration of such magnificent water routes as the Chesapeake Bay, Texas Gulf Coast, and Nile River. The adventures will engage you in the cultures, landscapes, and peoples that comprise these river valleys, coastal plains, and archipelagos. Your program will come alive as your vessel cruises among the islands, inlets, canals, and port cities that make up your excursion.

The educational and travel value of Elderhostel programs is tremendous. The program cost includes tuition for all courses, field trips, meals, accommodations, gratuities, port taxes, and the Elderhostel supplemental accident/illness/baggage insurance coverage. Also, for international programs, the cost includes round-trip airfare to and from your program destination

This is the first in a series of three to be published annually that will provide you with a detailed look at these special opportunities for discovery and adventure. **Space is limited, so please review the following pages, and click on the desired program number to register.**

Many of Elderhostel's catalogs can be accessed online, such as the Elderhostel Adventures Afloat catalog. This catalog contains descriptions of educational trips that are held anywhere from the Chesapeake Bay to the Nile River.

ELDERTREKS

www.eldertreks.com

E-mail: Click on the Contact Us link or send an e-mail to eldertreks@eldertreks.com

ElderTreks' Web site contains a lot of good information about trips geared specifically toward the 50-or-older traveler. This company specializes in adventure travel. In other words, the trips you'll find at this site aren't designed for people who like to be pampered while on vacation.

On ElderTreks' home page you'll see a post filled with signs to destinations such as Central Asia, Africa, Europe, the Americas, the South Pacific, Southeast Asia, and Asia Minor and the Middle East. If you click on a sign destination, you'll link to a Web page that describes all of the trips that are currently offered in that region. You'll also find information about the cost, the length of stay, and where travelers will arrive and depart on each trip. Some trips give travelers the option of extending their stay.

If you're having trouble deciding which trip sounds most interesting, click on a few of the photo library links you'll find throughout this section. Each photo library is filled with pictures of things other travelers have seen and experienced on their journey.

ElderTreks also provides several options for single travelers. To learn about these options, click on **All About ElderTreks**, and then link to **The Experience**. In this section you'll also find the answers to many frequently asked questions about ElderTreks vacation packages. This is the place to get answers about accommodations, food, guides, and exactly what's included in an all-inclusive package.

To see what vacation packages are coming up in the near future, or to read about ElderTreks Exploratory Trips, click on the **Highlighted Departures** link in the main menu bar. Exploratory Trips are more adventurous because elements of the trip are established as you go. These tours are geared toward people who like spontaneity, less structure, and more time to explore.

For example, The Amazon & Pantanal Exploratory Trip takes travelers through the vast forests, swamps, and waterways that cover Brazil. This trip is filled with opportunities to hike and explore the rivers, swamps, and jungles found in these regions.

Finally, to see how former ElderTreks participants have rated their experience, click on **Our Travelers and the Media Speak Out** and **Postcards from the Edge**. If you've never traveled off the beaten path, you may want to do just that after reading a few of the travel stories found in these sections.

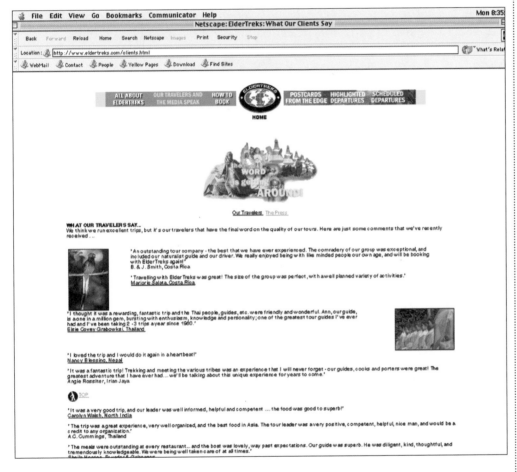

*This Web page, entitled **Our Travelers and the Media Speak Out**, contains comments written by travelers who have returned from an ElderTreks trip and wanted to share their experiences with others.*

Golden Escapes

www.goldenescapes.com

E-mail: admin@goldenescapes.com

You'll want to be sure to check out Golden Escapes' Web site, which contains a wealth of programs designed for travelers aged 50 and older. A Canadian-based company, Golden Escapes has been operating group tours since 1977.

To begin looking for a tour, click on the **The Tours** link on the home page. You'll link to a page that divides trips by season and location. Most of Golden Escapes' excursion packages are geared toward travelers interested in North America and the Pacific Islands; Britain, France, and Holland; or the Mediterranean. You can also find links for ecotours in Costa Rica, tours of castles and manor homes in England, or Golden Escapes' Greek Island-hopping excursions. Several other links are geared to those interested in traveling around a holiday.

You'll need to link to the descriptions of various tours to view pricing information for each trip. When you do, you'll notice the departure cities listed are in Canada, and the prices quoted are in Canadian dollars. To find out the price of these excursions in U.S. dollars and make travel arrangements from your city, either e-mail Golden Escapes (admin@goldenescapes.com) or call their toll-free phone number, which is listed at the bottom of every Web page. The company's mailing address and an online request form also can be found by clicking on the **Info Request** link.

Before leaving this section of the site, be sure to check out the link to **Terms & Conditions & General Information**. This section contains information about what the company covers and what it doesn't offer while you're traveling, how to file a complaint if you have one, information for those traveling alone, cancellation penalties, baggage allowances, passport information, and more.

Throughout the site, you will notice a link to **Golden Escapes' Back-Roads Touring** program. Although these tours aren't focused on 50-or-older travelers, they're still worth checking out if you're the type of tourist who enjoys traveling in a small group. These tours, most of which run 11 days or more, explore the back roads of places throughout England, Wales, Scotland, the Channel Islands, France, and Ireland. Several minitours, which run approximately four

days, are offered to travelers as well. Before leaving this section, you also might want to take a little time to read the comments written by former Back-Roads Touring program travelers.

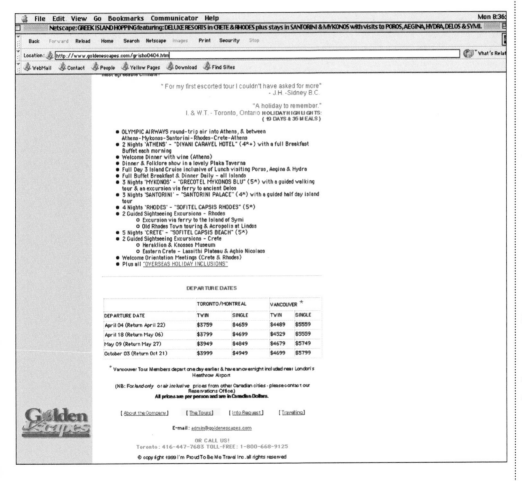

Golden Escapes is a Canadian company, and the prices for trips are listed in Canadian dollars. To get pricing and departure information for the United States, you'll need to contact Golden Escapes directly by clicking on the **Info Request** *link or calling the toll-free phone number posted on each Web page.*

BEDANDBREAKFAST.COM

www.bedandbreakfast.com

E-mail: Click on Feedback.

This site claims, "You're a click away from your getaway." OK, maybe it takes more than one click to find the perfect getaway, but bed-and-breakfast lovers will definitely want to add this site to their list of favorites.

Traveler Eric Goldreyer founded this site for other bed-and-breakfast lovers, and he has succeeded in providing them with a single, comprehensive, user-friendly source of information. This site contains information about more than 23,000 bed-and-breakfasts and inns located throughout the United States and overseas. You can make reservations online, e-mail innkeepers, and post questions and comments about a bed-and-breakfast or inn where you've stayed.

This site makes it easy to find accommodations at your intended destination. You can click on a world map or enter the city you plan to visit in the site's internal search engine. Next, you'll view a list of properties submitted by bed-and-breakfast and inn owners. Having the owner submit this information ensures that it is both accurate and up to date.

As you view these properties, you'll notice a list that gives the driving distance to nearby towns and cities. This information is really helpful if you plan to sightsee in the area. You also can access a map of the area and get directions to places you plan to visit by entering the inn's street address.

The best thing about this site, however, is the amount of detailed information it provides about each bed-and-breakfast or inn. You can read a description of the place you'll be staying, get a phone number and address, view pictures, and find out the price range of rooms. You also can see what amenities are offered, find out what activities are offered on-site or nearby, or read a review of the place from someone who has stayed there. If you're really hooked, you can go ahead and request a reservation online.

This site also sells gift certificates that can be used at more than 500 bed-and-breakfasts and inns located nationwide. Another link not to be missed lists all the special deals currently available on featured bed-and-breakfasts and inns located domestically and abroad. This feature allows you to search by state or country, or you can look for last-minute specials and package deals.

This screen shows a list of inns and bed-and-breakfasts where you can stay in Branson, Missouri, a favored vacation spot among senior travelers. You can read a short description of each accommodation, view photos, get room rates, and request a reservation online.

Chapter 9
Financial Resources

HOOVER'S ONLINE: THE BUSINESS NETWORK
www.hoovers.com

E-mail: Link to the Customer Support E-mail Form.

The Web has gone a long way toward putting the individual investor on the same footing as large financial institutions. Masses of research, which once were very expensive or not widely available, are now just a few mouse clicks away. Much of this information is available for free. Some sites, such as Hoover's Online: The Business Network, are semicommercial. This Web site is the brainchild of entrepreneur Gary Hoover. Hoover created a book containing easy-to-read overviews of the world's most important companies. The book was a hit, and in 1995 the company launched Hoover's Online, which has since evolved to become Hoover's Online: The Business Network.

Those who visit this Web site can find information about more than 14,000 public and private enterprises located worldwide. Hoover's 100,000 subscribers, who pay $14.95 per month, can access more in-depth information about many of these companies. (You'll notice that a key appears next to links at this site that can be accessed by members only.)

Even if you're not a member, you can register with this site for free and establish an online portfolio. If you're new to investing, you can get your feet wet by playing **Hoover's Stock Challenge**, which allows you to create your own fantasy stock portfolio online and compete against other players.

One of the better features of Hoover's Online is its extensive information about initial public offerings (IPOs). Visitors also can sign up to receive a free weekly update from **Hoover's IPO Central**, which shows IPO filings, pricing, and offerings scheduled for the coming week.

If you're shopping for a new insurance company, click on **YouDecide.com**, which can be found on the home page, to get side-by-side quotes from top-rated insurance companies. Hoover's also contains a database that allows visitors to search for mortgage rates online.

Link to **Hoover's List of Lists** to see how others rank companies and to get more information about key players in business and industry. You'll also find lists that rank companies by size, sales, reputation, and other criteria.

Newshounds can click on the **News Center** link to get the latest company, market, and IPO news. This section contains news links to a wide variety of publications, such as wire services and online financial magazines, newsletters, and journals.

Finally, if you can't find what you're looking for, try using the site's search engine, which allows visitors to search by company, keyword, or ticker symbol. You also can search for people, news, IPOs, and quotes.

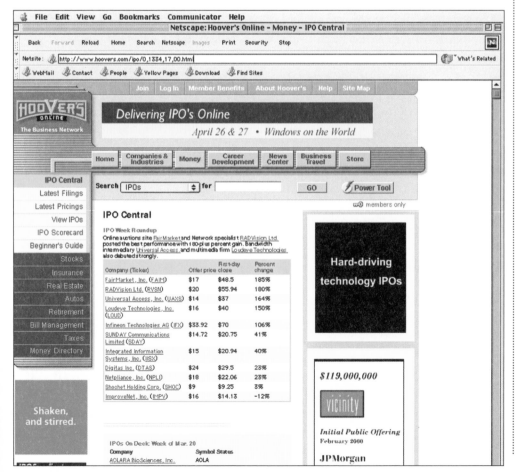

Hoover's IPO Central gives visitors the latest filing, pricing, and market information. You also can find out which companies' IPOs are scheduled to be offered in the coming week.

MORNINGSTAR

www.morningstar.com

E-mail: Click on the Contact Morningstar link found at the bottom of every Web page.

Morningstar is a must-visit site for investors. This company's Web site provides free, unbiased information on thousands of stocks and mutual funds. The **Tool Box** at this site is tremendous. Visitors can register for free with Morningstar and establish an online portfolio used to track and analyze their investments.

Two other interesting tools include a **Fund Selector** and a **Stock Selector**. The **Fund Selector** helps would-be investors scour Morningstar's database of more than 6,500 funds and then screen them. For additional information, link to the **Fund Center**, where you'll find **Real-Time Fund Analyses**, **Analysts' Picks**, **News**, and links to conversations about such funds as Janus, Vanguard 500 Index, Fidelity, and more. Remember, if you've registered with the site you can post messages to any of these lively, ongoing bulletin board conversations.

Morningstar's **Stock Selector** lets visitors screen an online database of more than 7,000 stocks. Linking to the **Stock Center** yields still more information.

Morningstar's **News** link contains information from popular market columnists as well as links to headline news. You also can find market graphs in this section, which can help you sum up the day's trading at a glance. An **Online University** contains links to help you get fiscally fit. This is the section to go to brush up on some investment basics. You also can find some articles and information aimed at women who want to start investing, or widows who suddenly find themselves in charge of the family's finances.

From the home page, you can link to access some of Morningstar's more popular reports on stocks and mutual funds. You also can link to read the company's most recent analyses of various stocks and mutual funds.

If you're feeling really brave, click on the **Annualizer** link in the **Tool Box** section. Enter what you paid for your stock, its current worth or amount you sold it for, and how long you owned it. Morningstar's **Annualizer** will show the total gain or loss and your annualized gain or loss.

Like many other financial sites, Morningstar offers some additional services for a fee. For $99 you can access Dow Jones Business news, do research on about 15,000 stocks and funds, and add X-Ray features to your portfolio. For

example, the **Style X-Ray** shows your portfolio's allocation to different investment strategies, while **World Regions X-Ray** analyzes your exposure to North American, European, Asian, and Latin American markets.

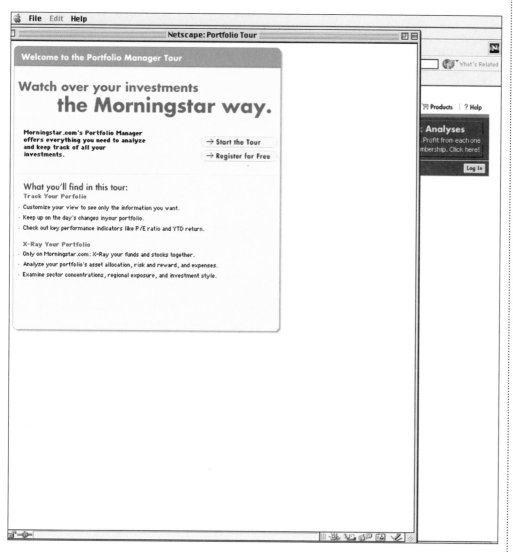

Interested in setting up a computerized portfolio? Take the **Portfolio Manager Tour**, which will show you how Morningstar can help you track and analyze your investments online.

MICROSOFT MONEYCENTRAL

http://moneycentral.msn.com/home.asp

E-mail: Click on the Feedback link.

Microsoft's MoneyCentral is the place to go for straightforward financial planning tools and advice. This well-rounded Web site contains quotes and charts for investors; financial news; tips to help you save money and manage debt; retirement planning information; estate management tools and information about how to prepare a will; insurance, banking, and tax information; and more.

In the **Investor** section you can find tools and information that will allow you to research stocks and mutual funds. Microsoft also allows you to establish an online **Portfolio** to track your investments.

Microsoft's MoneyCentral contains lots of practical, step-by-step guides to financial planning. This screen shows the site's major sections along the left side of the Web page.

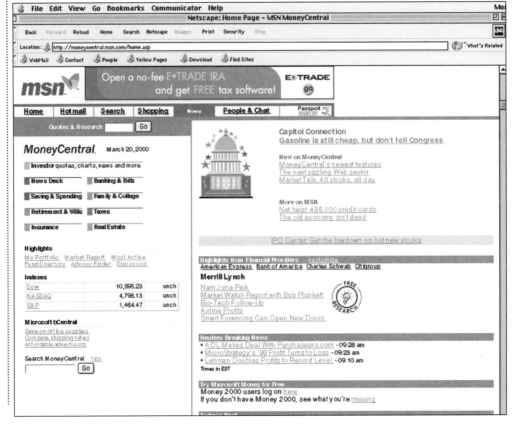

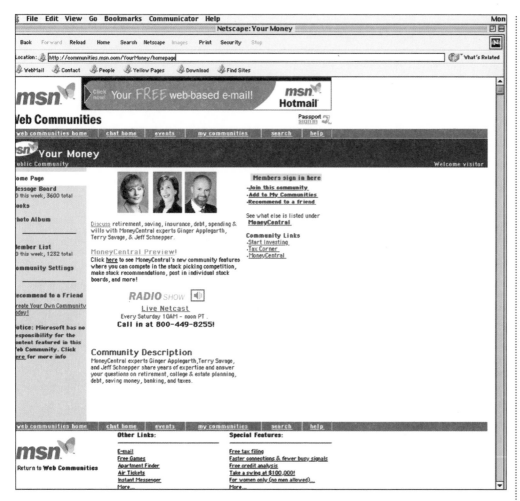

On MoneyCentral's bulletin boards you can query money experts Ginger Applegarth, Terry Savage, and Jeff Schnepper on topics such as retirement, savings, spending, estate planning, and wills.

The **News Desk** contains breaking news from the wire service Reuters, and financial articles of interest from magazines and newspapers. Visitors also can link to columns written by MoneyCentral's experts.

If you're looking for a quick reference guide to budgeting, car buying, debt, or fraud, click on **Saving & Spending**. This section also contains several handy tools, such as a debt evaluator, spending quiz, savings calculator, and debt consolidator.

You can find a step-by-step guide for retirement planning, estate management, and preparing a will in the **Retirement and Wills** section. Of particular interest in this section are the Quick Reference links that cover **Living Trusts**, **Medicare**, and **Social Security**. In each of these sections, you can view

*The **Retirement** section contains news articles of interest to seniors; step-by-step guides for retirement planning, estate planning, and preparing a will; and quick overviews of annuities, investing, living trusts, Medicare, Social Security, and tax issues.*

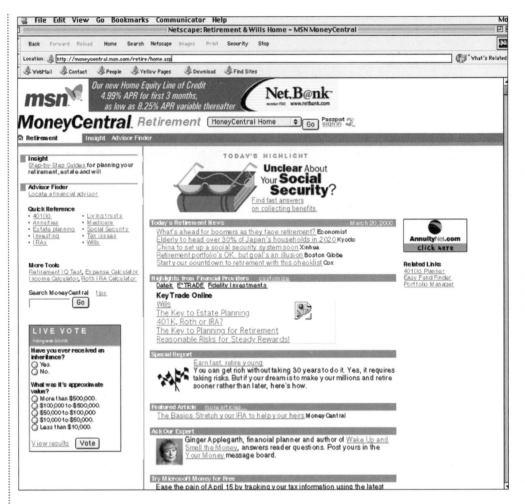

frequently asked questions and answers, access tools and articles, or see a list of related Web sites you can link to with a click of the mouse.

The **Insurance** section contains a number of guides to help you find the right amount of life, health, and property coverage. Be sure to check out the Quick Reference guide on long-term care. Many of the news stories found in this section also are geared toward older adults.

Those who are curious about the ins and outs of paying bills online can link to **Banking & Bills**. This section also contains a lot of good information about how to prevent credit card fraud.

Although your kids may be grown and no longer live at home, several items of interest to seniors can be found in the **Family & College** section. Of particular interest are the Quick Reference guides to death, divorce, and marriage. In these guides, you'll find the answers to questions such as:

▶ How does the death of a spouse affect the surviving spouse's insurance coverage?

▶ My husband died recently. How should I handle the bills that are coming in addressed to him?

▶ How will a divorce affect my estate planning?

▶ Can I lose my Medicare coverage if I get divorced?

▶ Will I lose the survivor benefit I collect from Social Security if I remarry?

In **Taxes**, you can find a tax estimator and several step-by-step guides to help you reduce and prepare your taxes, and a link that covers changes in tax law. There's also an excellent question-and-answer section on retirement plans.

If you own a second home or are thinking about relocating when you retire, be sure to visit the **Real Estate** section of MoneyCentral. You'll find tools that will let you calculate how much you can borrow, search for a home by ZIP code and price range, and check the crime rate in the area where you might move.

Snowbirds also can find an apartment and rental guide. This guide can help you narrow your search before you get to the area where you'll be spending the winter.

THE MOTLEY FOOL

www.fool.com

E-mail: Click on Contact Us.

Sometimes writers develop a Web site to promote themselves or their previous work. David and Tom Gardner are probably the only two people who started a Web site and then wrote a book to promote themselves. If you like talking shop in a festive atmosphere, you'll like The Motley Fool. Although the atmosphere is laid back, it's the advice that keeps people coming back.

When you first visit this site, take a moment to take the tour. It will not only give you a good overview of the resources you'll find here and tips for navigating the site, it will give you a flavor for the "fools" that run it.

To learn some investing basics, click on the link that will take you to **Fool's School**. You'll learn the "13 steps to foolish investing" and a lot of other good information aimed at beginners. The **Personal Finance** section also includes good tips and strategies. You can find links to stock strategies, financial news, and commentaries, or you can start your own online portfolio. Those who register (for free) with The Motley Fool can create multiple portfolios and track them against the S&P 500. Or you can follow stocks you own or stocks you just want to watch.

The **Quotes & Data** link allows you to get a wealth of information about stocks you're interested in with just a few clicks of the mouse. You can get a simple quote, a detailed quote that shows the 52-week high and low, news about the stock, analysts' earning estimates, and a snapshot of how the company is performing as a whole, or you can link to view a chart that shows the stock's price movements.

The **My Fool** link allows registered members to customize their financial information. You can view your favorite message boards and portfolios and change your preferences all on one page.

The Motley Fool's message boards are some of the most popular boards on the Web. You can share your opinion about a stock or ask a staff member a question. Remember, in this environment no question is considered foolish. In fact, many of the questions you'll see posted concern fundamental investment concepts. Even if you don't know a lot about investing, it's fun to jump on the bulletin board bandwagon and mock the "wise men of Wall Street."

File Edit View Go Bookmarks Communicator Help   Mo

Netscape: TMF: The Best of the Boards

Back Forward Reload Home Search Netscape Images Print Security Stop

Location: http://boards.fool.com/TopBoards.asp   What's Related

WebMail   Contact   People   Yellow Pages   Download   Find Sites

HOME   DISCUSSION BOARDS   QUOTES & DATA   STOCK RESEARCH   SHOP FOOLMART   MY PORTFOLIO   MY FOOL   LOGIN

FOLDERS • BEST OF • FAVORITES & REPLIES • CUSTOMIZE • HELP

Fool.com
Message Boards   SEARCH   Quick Find

Top Boards

1. Show me the [25] Most Recommended Posts

Recommended Posts

2. In [All Folders] Or In Just the [   ] Ticker

Recent Interviews

3. Posted ● Last 24 hours ○ Last 7 Days ○ From [3/6/00] To [3/20/00]

4. (GO)

Recommended Post	Recs	Board	Author	Date
Scientific American August 1998	28	Celera	mwidawer	3/19/00 1:26 PM
proto-FAQ: BRK vs. tech investing	26	Berkshire Hathaway	Rubic	3/19/00 1:27 PM
On weak form efficiency	18	Echelon Corporation	howardroark	3/19/00 5:19 PM
Re: The Internet Is Running Out Of Money	17	CMGI, Inc.	fredmaya	3/19/00 2:02 PM
Re: March 18 economist article	16	Celera	FushiTarazu	3/19/00 10:18 PM
OT - People defecting from this board	16	Living Below Your Means	gummipeach	3/19/00 9:26 PM
Biggest Compliment	15	Excite@Home	buckwheat66	3/19/00 8:51 PM
Don't Take My Money!	15	Living Below Your Means	CarlosMerighe	3/19/00 5:12 PM
Rambus & DDR RAM	14	Apple	ChicagoBob	3/19/00 2:18 PM
Rat's Voicemail	13	Rat's Broadband Bandwagon	OtterPater	3/19/00 8:58 PM
How will open access affect E@H?	13	Excite@Home	ojanen	3/19/00 5:55 PM
What Celera Can Sell: RTQ	12	Celera	YinOrdinaire	3/19/00 6:09 PM
Re: exchange on QCOM board	12	Nokia Corporation	tero	3/19/00 11:56 AM
Re: barron's list of co's running out of cash	12	Healtheon/WebMD	john126	3/19/00 11:26 AM
Re: XBox article	11	Rambus, Inc.	TinkerShaw	3/19/00 5:06 PM
Re: Mac User Percentage	10	Apple	aaashby	3/19/00 8:45 PM
Celera, genomics, and public perception	10	Celera	JDBarron	3/19/00 4:16 PM
Why Pharmas will subscribe (long)	10	Celera	humgenome	3/19/00 11:58 AM
Re: Next-Level Options Topic 2: The Dreaded &quo	10	Mechanical Investing	Rayvt	3/19/00 11:47 AM
Fortune mag on dot-coms	9	Berkshire Hathaway	UsuallyReasonabl	3/19/00 10:59 PM
Re: What happens if Portland announces free acce	9	Excite@Home	Pike51	3/19/00 5:00 PM
Re: We are a predictable lot	9	Celera	iseek2	3/19/00 10:35 AM
It's not just the money...	8	Celera	2158wca	3/19/00 11:24 AM
Re: FDWBaltimore	8	Berkshire Hathaway	FDWBaltimore	3/19/00 9:04 PM
RB Summary for Puma (long)	8	Puma Technology, Inc.	xerohype	3/19/00 1:19 PM

Stock Folders: A B C D E F G H I J K L M N O P Q R S T U V W X Y Z

The Motley Fool's message boards are among the most popular found on the Web. You can access information posted on a specific topic, or review what has been posted on the top 25 most popular boards, as shown here.

E*TRADE

Web address: www.etrade.com

Fire your broker! OK, maybe that would be a hasty move. But after you see what E*Trade has to offer, you might just think about it.

Why are sites like E*Trade so popular? Because they empower investors. With a few clicks of the mouse, you can research and review a company's performance and then use E*Trade to invest in stocks, bonds, options, and initial public offerings (IPOs). You also will find more than 5,000 mutual funds in which you can invest.

Like a broker, E*Trade accepts all common types of orders, such as market and limit orders, stop and stop-limit orders, all-or-none (AON) orders, and good-til-canceled (GTC) orders. Best of all, E*Trade charges no per-order, handling, or account maintenance fees. Customers are charged a standard commission for each trade, and a small fee for any special services they request, such as sending a stock certificate or wiring funds. (To see a list of commission rates, go to the home page, click on **About E*Trade**, and then click on **Low Commissions & Rates**.)

E*Trade also offers a lot of freebies. If you register for free with E*Trade, you can get up to 100 free, real-time quotes a day and a free e-mail account. E*Trade's members get certain privileges, such as the ability to make trades, get instant stock alerts, and apply for IPOs. You can set up a cash account with a minimum initial deposit of $1,000. You also can set up a margin account, which allows you to increase your purchasing power by borrowing against your stocks or mutual funds, with certain provisions. The minimum initial deposit for a margin account is $2,000.

If you're an active investor, you might qualify for the free Power E*Trade service, which offers super-fast order entry, Nasdaq Level II quotes, priority customer service, and trades as low as $4.95, after rebate. Power-traders also get all their stock quotes in real time.

Be sure to check out E*Trade's **Retirement** link, which can be found on the home page under **Financial Services**. You'll find information and rules for Roth IRAs, and learn how you can consolidate several IRA accounts using E*Trade.

In the **Account Services** section you can get your positions and balances in real time, check the cash and margin balances in your account, request a cash transfer, download statements, and more. But if you're a little reluctant to jump right in and start trading online, you can always learn the ropes by linking to E*Trade's virtual stock trading contest.

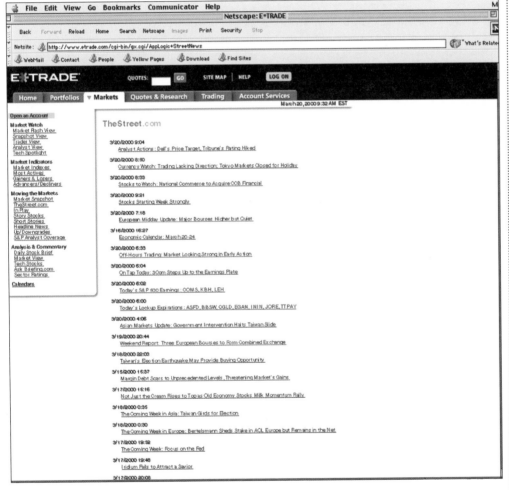

*E*Trade contains a link to TheStreet.com, one of the largest independent financial news organizations on the Web. The site reports breaking news and gives commentaries about what's happening in the market.*

Chapter 10
Hobbies

THE USGENWEB PROJECT

www.usgenweb.com

E-mail: webmaster@usgenweb.org

The USGenWeb Project is run by a group of volunteer genealogists located nationwide. This site contains links to every state and almost every county in the United States.

At the county level, amateur genealogists will find a wealth of information including a list of cemeteries, churches, townships, and land records. This section also contains several helpful links to additional resources on RootsWeb. In fact, The USGenWeb Project's Web site is hosted by RootsWeb.

The USGenWeb Project's state Web sites include helpful information as well, including family reunion bulletin boards, state histories, and maps showing how county boundaries within the state have changed over time. Many states also have ongoing projects, such as transcribing the rosters of Civil War regiments.

Because volunteers run the site, visitors will notice there's considerable variation among the state and county resources. However, all of the counties have links that allow visitors to post queries, access a state's home page, or access The USGenWeb Project's archives.

The USGenWeb Archives offers transcriptions of public domain records. Visitors can find copies of census records, marriage bonds, wills, and other public documents. The archives also contain links to other research projects that are underway.

Volunteers for the USGenWeb also are working to transcribe all of the U.S. Federal Censuses. Click on the **On-Line Inventory of Transcribed Census Links** to view the census reports already completed by volunteers. Other initiatives being undertaken include encouraging people to survey cemeteries and donate copies of their survey to The USGenWeb Project. Each state has its own cemetery registry that is broken down by county.

The USGenWeb's **Pension Project** provides transcripts of all pension-related materials for wars prior to 1900. This section also contains instructions for how to obtain pension records from the National Archives. The **Lineage Project** provides a place to list researchers who are looking for descendants of an ancestor who lived in the United States at one time and was born before December 31, 1850. These links include the ancestor's name, location, and dates, the e-mail address of the researcher, and the researcher's Web page about the family, if there is one.

Last but not least, check out the **Information for Researchers** link. This section contains many helpful tips for beginning researchers and answers to common problems and questions.

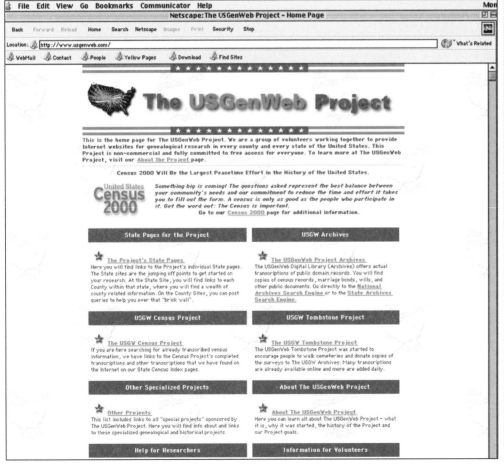

The USGen-Web's home page lists and describes the wide variety of genealogy projects being undertaken by this national network of research volunteers.

FOODTV.COM

www.foodtv.com

E-mail: ypaw@accuwx.com

Forget about buying a new cookbook. Hop on the Web and log on to FoodTV.com. Although this TV program doesn't air in every area of the country, you'll wish it did after you visit this Web site. In addition to getting recipes that have appeared on Food Network's television shows, you can view technique videos, search a culinary encyclopedia, get wine recommendations, learn about the latest cooking gadgets, and more.

Recently-aired recipes are listed under the name of each TV show on which they appeared. If the show doesn't air in your area, don't worry about it. When you link to a recipe, you see a number of videos you can watch that will review the finer points of how to make a particular dish.

Speaking of cooking videos, FoodTV.com has a well-rounded selection. These videos are really helpful because it's much easier to learn a particular cooking technique if you're shown how to do it. You can watch videos about everything from how to open a bottle of champagne to how to carve a turkey.

If you're surfing the Web using a 14- or 15-inch monitor, you'll appreciate the fact that the Web pages at this site are designed to fit your monitor size. This means you won't have to scroll from right to left to see information on any given page.

Another nice feature of FoodTV.com is that each recipe comes with suggestions for what to do to make it a complete meal. Better still, if you want to print out a recipe, click on the **printer-friendly version** button at the top of any recipe page. This will allow you to print out a simple black-and-white version, which will save on ink if you own a color printer.

If you can't find what you're looking for, use the site's internal search engine to sort through the more than 8,000 recipes stored at this site. You can search by show or time period, or by occasion, ingredient, preparation method, or taste preference.

Cooks who must prepare meals for picky eaters will appreciate FoodTV.com's **Menus of the Week** section, which can be found on the home page. You'll find an international meal, an easy-to-prepare meal, a sociable meal,

a light meal, a meatless meal, or one that's sure to please the carnivore in your family. Of course, no weekly menu plan would be complete without the hedonist's meal. The only thing missing at the end of this lard-laden meal is a link to several low fat recipes.

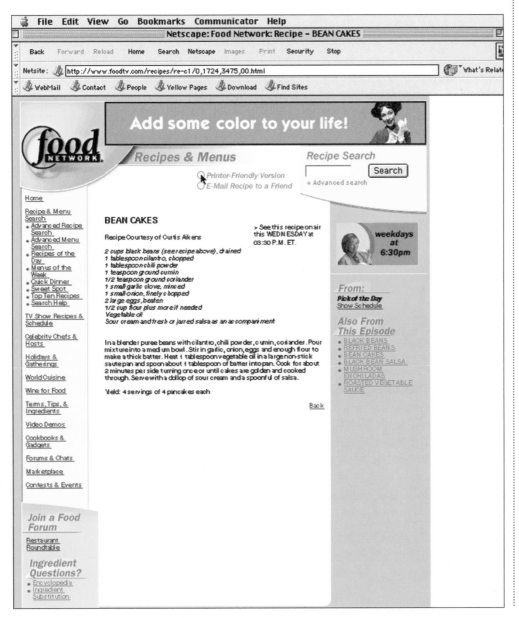

*Be sure to select the **printer-friendly version** when printing out a recipe at FoodTV.com's Web site. This "clean" version, which contains no Web page features, can be placed in a notebook or folder, allowing you to create your own cookbook of favorite recipes.*

CYNDI'S LIST

www.cyndislist.com

E-mail: cyndihow@oz.net

Cyndi's List contains more than 100 categories of information and 44,800 links to genealogy sites that are categorized and cross-referenced. This popular site, which is run by amateur genealogist Cyndi Howells, has been visited more than 12 million times since it was launched in 1996. The list of resources on the home page is overwhelming but impressive. Thankfully, Cyndi has taken the time to let visitors know which links were added recently.

Researchers have several different options for accessing information. You can search by topic or category, or use the site's internal search engine to find materials by keyword, surname, place name, or type of record. This site really gets you thinking about the thousands of people who do genealogy research as a hobby. It also brings home another important point. Chances are, you share a common ancestor with another amateur genealogist who has already researched your surname.

Rather than reinvent the wheel, try to locate the person or people who don't mind sharing their research. After all, you are family. In fact, rather than begin your research at this site, you might view it as the second or third resource you access while doing your research. Due to the mass of information you'll find at Cyndi's List, it's probably wise to visit this site after you've established a research objective.

For example, should you hook up with your long lost cousin, review the information they provide with a little bit of skepticism. Do they quote sources? Do they have official records that show the validity of their research? Chances are your cousin will help you up to a point. That's the time to start browsing Cyndi's list to verify the information you've been given.

Start by browsing Cyndi's List's **Category Index**. If you know which country your ancestors immigrated from, you can make your research all the way back to the old country go a lot faster by clicking on the name of the country to access resources from that area.

Other genealogy projects are harder to research. However, you can find links to genealogy resources for African Americans, adoptees, Native Americans, and

more. Indeed, amateur genealogists can find a lot more than a list of links at this site. You can find research tips, search tools, and even learn how to set up your own genealogy home page.

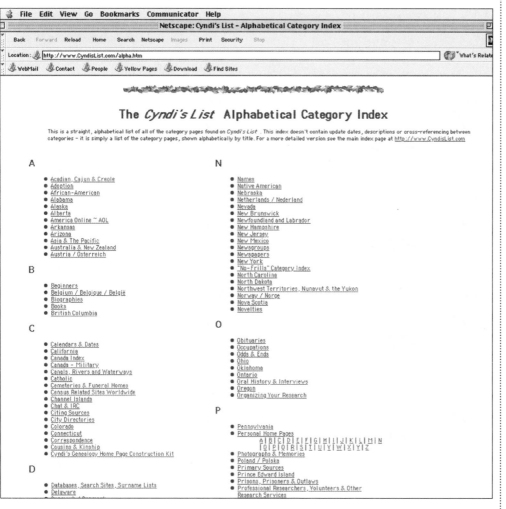

File Edit View Go Bookmarks Communicator Help

Netscape: Cyndi's List – Alphabetical Category Index

Back Forward Reload Home Search Netscape Images Print Security Stop

Location: http://www.CyndisList.com/alpha.htm   What's Related

WebMail Contact People Yellow Pages Download Find Sites

The *Cyndi's List* Alphabetical Category Index

This is a straight, alphabetical list of all of the category pages found on *Cyndi's List* . This index doesn't contain update dates, descriptions or cross-referencing between categories – it is simply a list of the category pages, shown alphabetically by title. For a more detailed version see the main index page at http://www.CyndisList.com

A
- Acadian, Cajun & Creole
- Adoption
- African-American
- Alabama
- Alaska
- Alberta
- America Online ~ AOL
- Arkansas
- Arizona
- Asia & The Pacific
- Australia & New Zealand
- Austria / Österreich

B
- Beginners
- Belgium / Belgique / België
- Biographies
- Books
- British Columbia

C
- Calendars & Dates
- California
- Canada Index
- Canada – Military
- Canals, Rivers and Waterways
- Catholic
- Cemeteries & Funeral Homes
- Census Related Sites Worldwide
- Channel Islands
- Chat & IRC
- Citing Sources
- City Directories
- Colorado
- Connecticut
- Correspondence
- Cousins & Kinship
- Cyndi's Genealogy Home Page Construction Kit

D
- Databases, Search Sites, Surname Lists
- Delaware

N
- Names
- Native American
- Nebraska
- Netherlands / Nederland
- Nevada
- New Brunswick
- Newfoundland and Labrador
- New Hampshire
- New Jersey
- New Mexico
- Newsgroups
- Newspapers
- New York
- "No-Frills" Category Index
- North Carolina
- North Dakota
- Northwest Territories, Nunavut & the Yukon
- Norway / Norge
- Nova Scotia
- Novelties

O
- Obituaries
- Occupations
- Odds & Ends
- Ohio
- Oklahoma
- Ontario
- Oral History & Interviews
- Oregon
- Organizing Your Research

P
- Pennsylvania
- Personal Home Pages
  A | B | C | D | E | F | G | H | I | J | K | L | M | N
  | O | P | Q | R | S | T | U | V | W | X | Y | Z
- Photographs & Memories
- Poland / Polska
- Primary Sources
- Prince Edward Island
- Prisons, Prisoners & Outlaws
- Professional Researchers, Volunteers & Other Research Services

Cyndi's List contains an overwhelming number of links to genealogical resources. The **Category Index**, shown here, puts these resources in alphabetical order to make browsing easier. Visitors will also find the date the category was last updated and the number of links in each category (in parentheses).

MARTHA STEWART LIVING OMNIMEDIA
www.marthastewart.com

E-mail: Click on About MSLO.

Martha Stewart Living Omnimedia is one of the more popular Web sites among craftspeople. Visitors can find links to gardening projects, crafts, special occasions, cooking and entertaining, and more.

Like many Web sites, Martha Stewart's site works best if it is viewed with the latest version of Netscape Navigator, Microsoft Internet Explorer, or America Online's proprietary browser. If you are viewing the site using another browser, you might not be able to take advantage of some of the Web site's more advanced features, such as quicktime videos.

This site is divided into eight main sections. In several of these sections you'll find links to the **Meeting Place**. The **Meeting Place** allows crafters to exchange ideas on bulletin boards, meet and talk with members in live discussions, and participate in scheduled question-and-answer hours featuring Martha Stewart, editors from *Martha Stewart Living*, and some special guests.

You'll also find a list of projects Martha Stewart recently completed on her radio or TV show. If you click on **Transcripts** or **Program Guide**, you'll link to an online calendar. Select the day the project aired, click on the project, and you're in business. A handy list of additional ideas also accompanies each project.

The **Cooking & Entertaining** section is particularly good. This is the place to find answers and inspiration for everything from a large dinner party to a small get-together. A lot of fun stuff can be found in this section as well, such as the winners of Cookie of the Week.

This Web site is not without its commercial side, however. You'll find plenty of links throughout the site to purchase books, kits, and other products that bear Martha Stewart's name.

Regardless of where you purchase your craft materials, you'll find the directions for each of Stewart's projects to be clear, complete, and well organized. In the end, skilled crafters will wind up with a product that looks just like what they saw on TV. If you find you are all thumbs when it comes to crafts, you can still make sure your home looks good thanks to Martha By Mail. Link to the **Shopping** section where you'll find flowers, vases, and all sorts of products to give your home and garden that personal touch.

INTERNET

File   Edit   View   Go   Bookmarks   Communicator   Help   Mon 9:00:55 AM

Netscape: Martha Stewart Living

Back   Forward   Reload   Home   Search   Netscape   Images   Print   Security   Stop

Location: http://www.marthastewart.com/meeting_place/index.asp   What's Related

WebMail   Contact   People   Yellow Pages   Download   Find Sites

marthastewart.com MEETING PLACE   HOMEPAGE | HELP

bulletin boards   live discussions   q & a hours

Welcome to Meeting Place, where you can exchange ideas on Bulletin Boards, meet and talk with members in Live Discussions, and join our scheduled Q & A Hours, featuring myself, editors of Martha Stewart Living, and special guest experts. Whether you're planning a wedding, starting seeds for your garden, or looking for a new way to file your paperwork, Meeting Place is where to share great tips and make new friends.

Martha Stewart

bulletin boards

Post messages to other members, ask for advice, and exchange ideas with those who share your particular area of interest. Bulletin Boards are open 24 hours a day, 7 days a week.

Please visit your main area of interest below, where you will find specific Bulletin Board topics.

COOKING & ENTERTAINING
HOME
HOLIDAYS
CRAFTS
KEEPING
GARDENING
WEDDINGS

q & a hours

Talk with Martha or one of our experts

Tuesday, March 21 | 4 P.M. EDT
WHAT TO HAVE FOR DINNER: QUICK MEALS AFTER WORK
Join our food editors to learn some quick solutions to the problem of making dinner after a long day.

Thursday, March 23 | 1 P.M. EDT
WEDDINGS: ATTIRE FOR THE MOTHER OF THE BRIDE
For all those mothers whose daughters are soon to be wed, Martha Stewart weddings editors and a guest designer will offer advice at this Q & A on selecting the best attire for the special day.

[CALENDAR]   [TRANSCRIPTS]

live discussions

Talk with other members live every day from 10 A.M. to 10 P.M. EDT. Please select a topic below to enter a discussion.

BLUE-RIBBON ASSOCIATIONS

To ensure that you get the best and most accurate information possible, we've established partnerships with members of top professional associations who will visit Meeting Place regularly and offer expert advice on your questions. We call these partners our Blue-Ribbon Associations.

AMERICAN FEDERATION OF MUSICIANS
AMERICAN GEM SOCIETY
AMERICAN HUMANE ASSOCIATION
AMERICAN SEWING GUILD
FRENCH CULINARY INSTITUTE
HOME SEWING ASSOCIATION
INTERNATIONAL GUILD OF GLASS ARTISTS
NATIONAL CRAFT ASSOCIATION
NATIONAL GARDENING ASSOCIATION
PAINTING AND DECORATING CONTRACTORS OF AMERICA
WEDDING & PORTRAIT PHOTOGRAPHERS INTERNATIONAL

---

*The **Meeting Place** gives visitors a forum for exchanging ideas. You can post a message on one of the online bulletin boards, meet and talk with other members in live discussions, or participate in scheduled question-and-answer sessions that feature Martha Stewart or other crafts-people.*

BETTER HOMES & GARDENS

www.bhg.com

E-mail: Click on Contact the Editors.

B*etter Homes & Gardens* magazine has been around for years. Now, thanks to the Web, you can access some of the newest and best features of this magazine online.

Visitors can find links to home decorating, recipes, ideas for the garden, craft projects, and more. In the **House & Home** section, you'll find a link to the **Kitchen Planning Guide**. The kitchen and the bathroom are usually the first rooms to get remodeled in an older home, and this guide contains all the tools you'll need to get started.

Click on the **Home Improvement Encyclopedia** link in this section to access home repair and improvement advice. You will find information on wiring, plumbing, carpentry, decks, and masonry and concrete. Better still are the **Project Calculators** that help take the guesswork out of the home improvement experience.

Other links of interest in the **House & Home** section include guides for decorating every room in your home, online home plans, and several wood plan projects you can download to your computer, courtesy of *Wood* magazine.

In the **Food/Recipes** section you can get information on everything from how to build a gingerbread house to setting a beautiful table. A wide variety of recipes and an online cooking encyclopedia also can be found. While here, be sure to link to the **Menu Planner**. This handy little tool allows visitors to mix and match seasonal menus with a few clicks of the mouse.

Those who like to putter around the yard are sure to appreciate the **Gardening** section. You can find out what's new in the *Better Homes & Gardens* "test" garden, review some tried-and-true garden plans, and access a guide about when to plant spring bulbs.

If you're feeling a little "crafty," visit the **Crafts** section. You'll find instructions for many different craft projects that you can buy and download to your computer. (*Better Homes & Gardens* gives instructions for how to download and print out various projects.) This section contains links to wood-crafting techniques, the basics of knitting, and more. Quilters and cross-stitchers also will find a lot of useful information in this section, such as the cross-stitch calculator that can help you determine the finished size of a pattern.

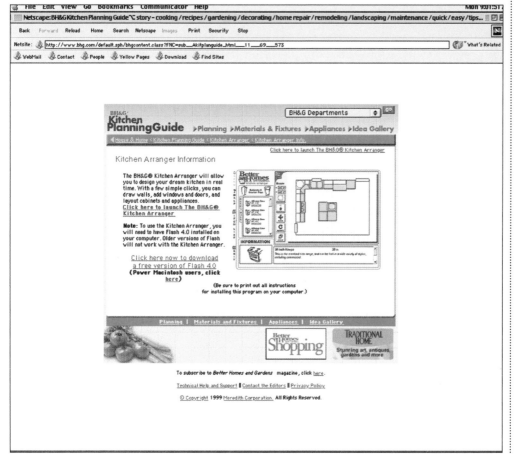

Better Homes & Gardens' *Web site contains a* **Kitchen Arranger**, *which allows visitors to design their kitchen right on their computer screen. You can draw walls, add windows and doors, and lay out cabinets and appliances.*

THE PET CHANNEL

www.thepetchannel.com

E-mail: info@thepetchannel.com

Pets are like family members to most folks. At The Pet Channel, you'll find all kinds of resources to keep your pet healthy and happy. The **Health** section allows visitors to ask a vet a question. You also can scan the questions and answers of some common problems or print out informative articles on health topics ranging from flea control to pet diabetes.

If the dog is driving you nuts, click on **Training** to get advice from a qualified animal trainer. The Pet Channel has a variety of trainers who specialize in training dogs, cats, and horses.

The products in the **Shopping** section range from unusual to downright hilarious. If you need a good laugh, check out the link to **Kitty Safari**. For $19.95, you can occupy your cats by playing a video of birds, mice, and squirrels. According to The Pet Channel, some cats even start pawing at the TV screen.

Click on **Find a Pet** to link to The Pet Channel's shelter and rescue center. This searchable database can help you find animal shelters and humane societies in your area. Complete a short questionnaire, and you'll get an online recommendation for a suitable breed of dog or cat. If you already know what you want, link to the database in this section to find the name of a breeder.

In **Fun Stuff**, you'll find book reviews, cartoons, a picture gallery of pets, and a link to **In the Dog House**, which chronicles The Pet Channel Correspondent Irene O'Brien's life with her Labrador.

The **Forums** section gives owners a good place to vent about their pet's latest reign of terror, or post a funny story about their pet's newest escapade. This section of the site is definitely favored by dog lovers. You also can find posts written by people who have adopted and raised everything from squirrels to skunks, or talk with other animal lovers in one of the site's chat rooms. Unlike some Web sites, you don't have to register with The Pet Channel to participate in a chat.

Other links allow you to get your pet's horoscope or see when a renowned vet is scheduled to participate in the next online chat. You also can register your pet or sign up for The Pet Channel's free e-mail newsletter.

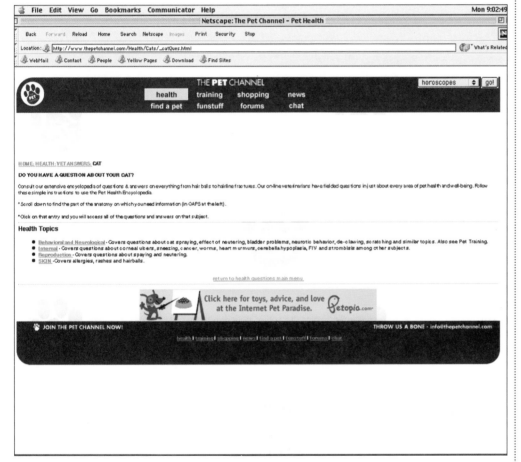

*In the **Health** section of The Pet Channel, visitors will find veterinarians' answers to many of the common problems and concerns faced by pet owners.*

EPICURIOUS

http://food.epicurious.com

E-mail: Click on the Help link.

Serious cooks will love Epicurious, which contains more than 10,000 recipes from *Gourmet* and *Bon Appetit* magazines. From the home page, visitors can link to the Big Three: **Eating**, **Drinking**, and **Playing with Your Food**.

The **Eating** section contains a link to **Recipes**. Once in **Recipes**, you can search the site's entire database for a tasty dish, or you can sort by category, such as desserts. In the **Ingredients** section you can get tips on how to buy the freshest seasonal ingredients. You'll also find several guides to restaurants located both domestically and abroad. Another link of interest allows you to search for out-of-print cookbooks. If the cover is falling off an older cookbook you own and you haven't found a replacement, look here.

Basic cooking techniques are covered in the **Basics** section. You'll also find links to several online videos that cover the basics. The videos are interesting and fun to watch. They're great as an instruction tool for cooks, since certain skills, such as how to cut and filet a fish, can be learned faster if you watch the process. To watch any of these videos, you'll need a software program called RealPlayer. Epicurious provides a link so you can download this free program to your computer if you don't already have it.

Two other links in **Eating** allow you to search for international recipes or seasonal recipes, such as soft-shell crabs. You'll also find several cookbook recommendations in this section.

The **Drinking** section contains the usual cocktail recipes and wine and beer guides. There's even a link to some tried-and-true hangover cures. Clicking on **Playing with Your Food** will link you to several different forums where you can share dining experiences with others. There's even a link on how to eat "problem" foods—such as snails or corn-on-the-cob—in public.

Three other sections, **Epicurious TV**, **Gourmet**, and **Bon Appetit**, allow visitors to search for recipes they've seen on TV or in either cooking magazine. You will, of course, find links encouraging you to subscribe to either *Gourmet* or *Bon Appetit*.

A number of handy cooking tools can be referenced quickly, such as a dictionary of wine terms and a dictionary of more than 4,000 food terms. You'll also find a chart for converting metric measurements and another for converting

certain fresh herbs and spices into the dry seasoning equivalent. At this point, you're probably wondering what you'll use to cook all this good food. Click on the **Shopping** link to see what culinary tools you can find at Williams-Sonoma.

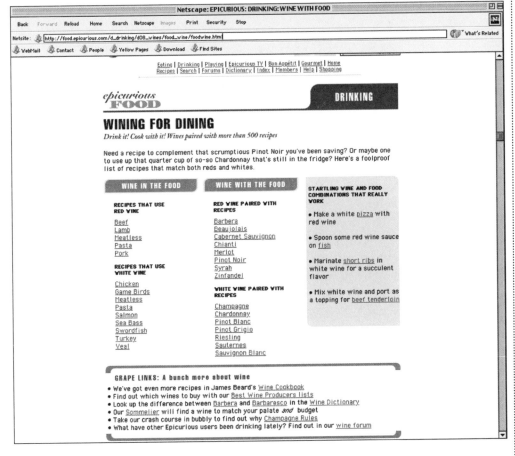

In addition to its recipes from Gourmet and Bon Appetit, those who visit Epicurious' Web site can get a wine recommendation or find recipes for dishes made with wine.

Chapter 11
Entertainment

CBS SPORTSLINE

www.cbssportsline.com

E-mail: support@sportsline.com

Ever wonder what the Sunday football commentator was talking about when he said you should log on and go to "CBS SportsLine dot com"? He was referring to the address of the station's Web site: *www.cbssportsline.com*.

At the top of this home page, you'll see four tabs that indicate the main categories found at this site: **U.S. Sports**, **Euro Sports**, **Fantasy**, and **Shop**. (Top tabs may change for different sport seasons.) Each contains several subcategories of information. You'll also find news stories, and you'll see a link to **Fast Facts** that gives you standings, schedules, and sports stats as well as information about teams, players, and injuries. Another link will take you directly to the scores you want.

All of these features are standard among sports Web sites. What really makes CBS SportsLine stand out, however, is that it allows you to create a personalized sports page to track your favorite sports teams and players with ease. This service is free to those who register with CBS SportsLine.

You also can set up a personal calendar for free. SportsLine's **Personal Calendar** allows you to keep track of your favorite sports teams, events, and exclusive CBS SportsLine events, such as live chats. You also can use the calendar to store appointments, announcements, and other personal reminders.

Another interesting feature of this site is the **Fantasy** link, which allows you to create different scenarios for your favorite teams and see the projected outcome. CBS SportsLine's Fantasy Editor Scott Engel also tackles a Fantasy Football topic every Wednesday during football season.

If you enjoy talking sports, be sure to check out the forums and chats. You can ask celebrities questions or post a message on any of the site's online chat boards, provided you register with the site. There are also several free e-mail newsletters you can sign up for.

Speaking of which, any visitor who signs up with CBS SportsLine automatically gets enrolled in SportsLine Rewards and starts earning points. You can earn points by viewing Web pages on the site, for example. After you've accumulated enough points, you can go on a shopping spree at CBS SportsLine's store.

This site also offers memberships in SportsLine Rewards Plus, which costs $39.95 a year. This service offers some extras, including the opportunity to earn more points. Only you can determine whether this service is worth your money.

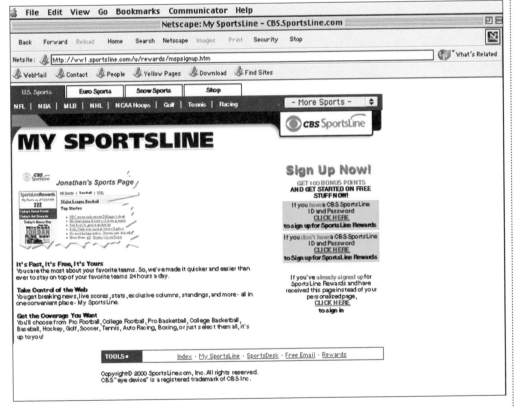

CBS SportsLine allows visitors to create a personal Web page. You can choose the teams you follow and select which news, scores, and player information you want to see.

ALL MOVIE GUIDE

www.allmovie.com

E-mail: Click on E-Mail Us.

Movie lovers are sure to enjoy the All Movie Guide. This site's home page gives you all the current movie information available. You can find out what movies have recently hit the theaters and what movies will be released in coming months, see a list of the top ten videos, review a list of movies now out on video, and even find out what movies are playing on television that night.

The information you'll find at this site is comprehensive. You can read a plot synopsis, find the name of the director, get the film's rating, see what the movie critic deems to be the flick's best and worst qualities, and find the date of the film's release. You also can link to read profiles of the film's stars, see how the movie is faring at the box office, or see if the film contains any explicit language, violence, or sexual situations.

The All Movie Guide also gives you an opportunity to voice your opinions. After viewing a film, you can go back online and submit your ratings and comments.

It's pretty easy to find the movie review you're seeking at this site, even if the movie is fairly obscure. If you get stuck, you always can use the site's internal search engine, which allows you to search by actor or actress, plot line, movie, or keyword. You also can search by character, title, location, and other criteria. If you're not really sure what you're looking for, click on **Quick Browse** and search by movie genre. You also can find an extensive set of links to films produced in other countries, or browse for a movie by decade.

Would-be movie critics will make good use of the glossary of movie-related terms at this site. For example, the term animation brings up links to everything from animascope to claymation to digitizing. In addition, you can enter and search for the definition of an unfamiliar term.

Film fans can find essays about how various movie studios were founded and how they have changed over the years. You also can find out what characteristics make a film fall into a particular genre, such as cult films or avant-garde films.

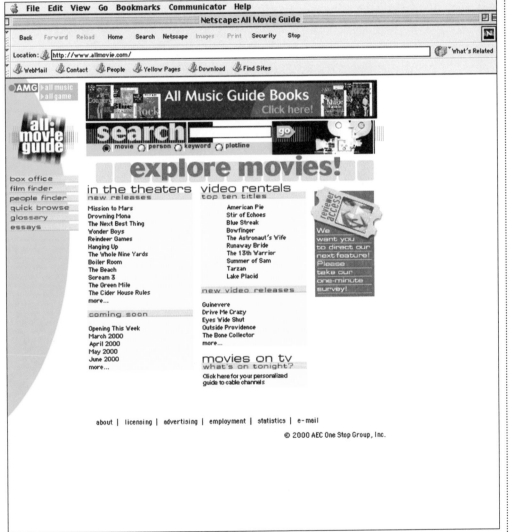

The All Movie Guide's home page contains the latest information about everything from big-screen movies to videos. The site's internal search engine allows you to look for a movie by title, person, keyword, or plot line.

CNN Sports Illustrated

www.cnnsi.com

E-mail: cnnsi@cnnsi.com

CNN Sports Illustrated combines the assets of CNN news with the expertise of the staff at *Sports Illustrated* magazine. The result: a 24-hour sports news Web site that is jammed with up-to-the-minute information.

Visitors can access breaking news stories, scores, statistics, highlights, interviews, analysis, and commentary by some of the best sports journalists in the world. The images at this site aren't shabby either; many of the pictures are taken by photographers for *Sports Illustrated*.

At this site, you can find news about U.S. baseball, pro football, college football, pro basketball, men's and women's college basketball, hockey, golf, tennis, soccer, and more. You also can link to get local sports news for more than 150 cities throughout the United States.

The coverage in the **World Sports** section could be beefed up a little. Soccer fans, however, will be pleased with the quantity and quality of information they'll find if they click on the **World Soccer Top 10** link. Throughout CNN Sports Illustrated, you'll find links to audio clips and video clips. News junkies also can sign up to receive *Sports Today*, CNN Sports Illustrated's daily e-mail newsletter. This free newsletter summarizes the day's top stories, refers readers to new links on the site, and includes game analysis from the staff at *Sports Illustrated*.

Sports fans will love the message boards at this site. To post a message, however, you'll need to complete the site's free registration process. You also can fire off a question to columnists at *Sports Illustrated*, take part in a poll about a sporting event, or **Sound Off** about the athletes and teams who are making the headlines.

Fantasy Central is another popular feature at CNN Sports Illustrated. During football season, for example, the site hosts several free Fantasy Football games. You also can try to beat the site's football experts or test your knowledge in the daily trivia blitz.

In addition, CNN Sports Illustrated has a travel link where you can find information about many sports-oriented vacations, such as international golf outings in the Irish countryside. You also can set up your own free e-mail

account or create a personalized CNN interactive home page that brings the sports, news, weather, and financial information you want to see right to your desktop.

You can also link to *Sports Illustrated*'s swimsuit issue, where you can browse the gallery, search for a model by name, or link to view issues dating back to 1996.

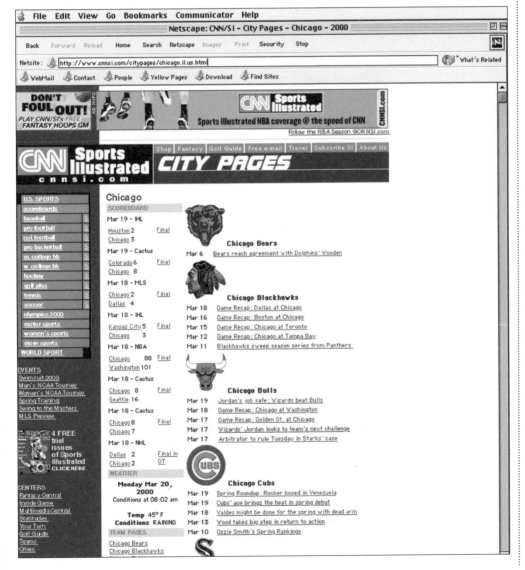

THE INTERNET MOVIE DATABASE

www.imdb.com

E-mail: help@imdb.com

Movie and video lovers are sure to enjoy The Internet Movie Database (IMDb). This site was started by movie fans for other movie fans. Although Amazon.com bought IMDb in 1998, the site's focus hasn't changed. Visitors can access information about more than 200,000 movies and TV shows made since 1892. You can find out who was in a particular film, who made it, awards the movie won, filming locations, and even reference famous quotes. Not only can you look up movies, you can get information about more than 400,000 actors and actresses and nearly 40,000 directors.

The home page contains information about special features, a movie of the day, news headlines, celebrity birthdays, trivia, and more. The site's main menu spans the top of the page. To find what you want quickly, use the internal search engine. This search engine allows you to search for titles, characters, people, quotes, biographies, and plots.

You can also browse for what you're seeking by section. The **What's Hot** section gives visitors information about the most popular movies in theaters and in video stores, the latest video releases, new movie-related books, movie soundtracks, and more.

The **Fun Features** section has all sorts of searchable databases. You can see which famous people share your birthday, what's playing at the theater nearby, what movies were filmed near you, and link to a list of favorite movies. You'll have ample opportunity to test your movie and TV knowledge in the **Games and Contest** section. If you score high enough on IMDb's Trivia game, your name gets entered in a weekly drawing for a cash prize.

Movie lovers will enjoy the **Message Boards**, which contain posts from people around the world. Anyone can browse and read messages. However, to post a message, you must first register (for free) with the site.

The **IMDb Recommends** section contains a database where you can get suggestions for movies. For example, entering the movie *Apollo 13* yields suggestions for movies such as *The Right Stuff*, *Forrest Gump*, *Titanic*, and other films. Parent company Amazon.com also gets a plug in this section. You'll be able to

see at a glance whether a recommended movie is available through Amazon.com in DVD or VHS. In addition, you'll be able to link to see if a recommended movie is playing at a theater near you.

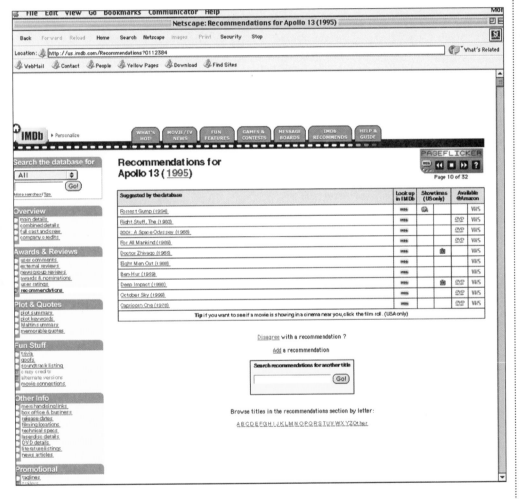

The Internet Movie Database allows visitors to search for other movies they might enjoy by entering the title of a movie they like. For example, entering the movie Apollo 13 generates recommendation for movies such as The Right Stuff and Forrest Gump.

CNET Gamecenter.com

www.gamecenter.com

E-mail: support@cnet.com

CNET Gamecenter.com proclaims it is "the ultimate gaming service." Given the selection and information you'll find at this site, it just might be. The site is organized like a subject tree. Electronic games are divided into categories, such as computer games or video games, and then subcategories, such as action or adventure.

The **Computer Games** category contains the majority of information you'll find at this site. You can see what new computer games were released this week, get a preview of soon-to-be-released games, get tips and link to strategy guides, or read a detailed review. If you're interested in purchasing the game, you can link to search for its price.

Before you do that, however, check out the freebies this site has to offer. Click on **Downloads**, which can be found at the bottom of every Web page. Next, click on the category you're interested in, such as puzzles, and browse through the list of available game titles. You can sort this list by game title, number of downloads, date, or other criteria. Each item on the list shows the game's title, a short description, the operating system (OS) needed to run the game, and the license. If you're like most people, you're working on a personal computer that uses Windows as its OS. Consequently, you'll only want to look at games that use the Windows operating system.

Next, check out the **License** for the game. You'll find there are three types of game licenses: free, shareware, and demos. Free games or freeware are yours for the taking. Shareware games are sold by individuals or companies for a nominal fee. Shareware programs are available on a limited-time basis (usually 30 to 60 days). If you decide to purchase a shareware game before it expires, you must register the software. Registration entitles you to users' manuals, support, and discounts on upgrades. Demo or demonstration games are similar to shareware games because they allow you to test-drive a game before you buy it. Demo games work for a limited time and may not include all the game's features.

If you're concerned about downloading a software program from the Internet, your concern is valid. CNET, however, has an outstanding reputation for providing glitch-free, virus-free software programs. (For a step-by-step guide to downloading programs, refer to this book's CD-ROM.)

File Edit View Go Bookmarks Communicator Help   Mo

Netscape: CNET.com – Downloads – PC – Games – Cards, Casino, Lottery

Back   Forward   Reload   Home   Search   Netscape   Images   Print   Security   Stop

Location: http://download.cnet.com/downloads/0,10150,0-10037-106-0-1-4,00.html   What's Related

WebMail   Contact   People   Yellow Pages   Download   Find Sites

CNET | News | Hardware | Downloads | Trends | Games | Jobs | Auctions | Prices | Tech Help   Free Email

CNET DOWNLOAD.COM   Search   [Go!]
                                                                   Advanced • Tips [In PC   ◆]

Backup Restore lost or deleted files in just one click!
Try @Backup Now! Free for 30 Days!
Easiest way to access and protect your data.

CNET | Downloads | PC | Games | Cards, Casino, Lottery

Found: 415 Displaying: 1-25   ‹Previous 1 2 3 4 5 6 7 8 9 10 11 12 13 14 15 16 17 Next›

Re-sort by Title	Buy	Pick	Date Added	Downloads	File Size
1000: Lots of Happiness in the Game 1.0 Have fun with this addictive card game with superb graphics. OS: Windows 95/98/NT License: Shareware			03/17/2000 NEW	563	4.6MB
BVS Solitaire Collection 2 S Play 130 different solitaire games. OS: Windows 95/98/NT License: Shareware			03/16/2000	883	1MB
Club Rio Casino 2.0 Have fun with this extensive selection of games on the Internet. OS: Windows 95/98/NT License: Free			03/16/2000 NEW	241	5.0MB
Virtual Fruit Machine 1.0 Pull the handle on this realistic, up-to-date simulation of a fruit machine. OS: Windows 95/98 License: Shareware			03/16/2000 NEW	343	3MB
CardGame? 1.0 Download this blackjack game. OS: Windows 95/98/NT License: Shareware			03/15/2000	247	1.1MB
HorseRacing 1.0 Bet on which horse will finish the race first. OS: Windows 95/98/NT License: Shareware			03/15/2000	384	844K
Pronp Loto Expert 2.0 Play the 6/49 lottery with fully optimized systems. OS: Windows 95/98/NT License: Shareware			03/15/2000 NEW	48	784K
Randy Keno 1.0 Try a Keno casino game. OS: Windows 95/98/NT License: Free			03/15/2000 NEW	114	1.6MB
interBet - Play Money Casino 2.22 Enjoy an online casino game where you play for iBux. OS: Windows 95/98/NT License: Shareware			03/14/2000 NEW	81	4.5MB

This screen shows you some of the games you can download from CNET's Gamecenter.com. You can sort by title, date added, or number of downloads. The OS the game uses is shown along with licensing information that indicates whether the program is free, shareware, or a demo version.

Chapter 12
News and Weather

MY VIRTUAL NEWSPAPER
http://www.refdesk.com/papmain.html

E-mail: rbdrudge@refdesk.com

You won't find a lot of original content at My Virtual Newspaper. However, you will find just about everything else at this award-winning Web site. My Virtual Newspaper, which is part of Refdesk.com, has links to every major wire service, newspaper, magazine, and sports Web site on the Internet. If that weren't enough, you can link to see streaming video of many of the day's top news stories.

When you log on to this site's home page, the first thing you'll notice is the headline news traveling across the page from The Wire, an Associated Press (AP) news service. You can satisfy your need for news by clicking on the ticker to view the entire story, or you can browse a bit first.

Just beneath the streaming headline news you will find links to all the major wire services, such as AFP, AP, CNN, Reuters, and UPI. You can link to see pictures from AP. There are also some news indexes, business news services, and clipping services that have a number of interesting features. For example, **The News Index** has a link so visitors with sight difficulties can enlarge the text size without distorting the page.

The link to listen to news from some major news stations is a little disappointing. Some of the news is out-of-date or impossible to access unless you have the software program Real Audio Player installed on your computer.

The real bread and butter of this site is its newspaper section. Online newspapers are grouped by state and country. Of the national online newspapers, *USA Today* and *The Washington Post* rank among the best. The list of foreign online newspapers is amazing. Those who can read another language can brush up on their language skills by linking to one of these newspapers.

Even if you don't know another language, do take time to read one of the international English-language newspapers. You'll find a number of articles that reveal what people in other nations think about American politics. Visitors also can find a seemingly endless list of national and worldwide news site links. If you can't find the news you're seeking at one of these sites, it probably hasn't happened yet.

At the top of the home page you'll notice a number of other links to online encyclopedias and reference material. Refdesk.com has a lot more to offer than just news and information. To find out what that includes, click on **Home** to access Refdesk.com's Web page.

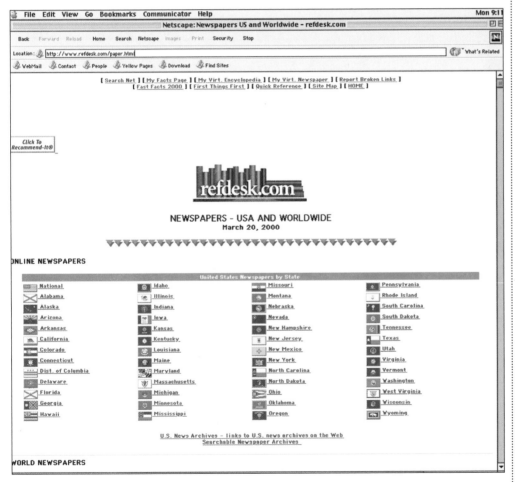

My Virtual Newspaper's Web site contains a lot more than links to online newspapers. Visitors also can access all of the major wire services and a large variety of online magazines.

ABCNEWS.COM

http://abcnews.go.com/

E-mail: Click on E-mail ABCNews.com.

Of the major TV networks with an online presence, ABC's Web site is one of the best. ABCNews.com is part of the Go Network, which is a combination search engine/Web portal.

Although the site is designed to be browsed, you can search by keyword using the Go Network's search engine. This search engine allows you to search ABCNews.com, ABC News on TV, or the entire Web. A link in the upper left corner of the home page allows you to get your local weather report. Once you've selected your city, ABCNews.com will send a "cookie" to your computer, which is a tiny data file that stores your information. The next time you visit ABCNews.com, the site will read the cookie and "recognize" you, and your local weather forecast will appear automatically.

A button for each news section at the site appears in the main menu bar along the left side of the page. At the end of the main menu you'll see links to all of ABC's news programs, such as *20/20*, *Nightline*, and *World News Now*. You'll also see a link to get local news from the ABC affiliate in your area. Other links of interest in the main menu bar include a link to the sports Web site ESPN.com, which also is part of the Go Network.

To help visitors, ABCNews.com shows headline news from each news category. This will save you time because you won't have to click on each news section in the main menu just to find information of interest. You also can get weather, local news, and e-mail alerts by registering with the site. E-mail news-alerts let registered users know about breaking news events. This service also keeps members up to date about enhancements to the site.

ABCNews.com's interactive features also are outstanding. You can take part in an ABC News poll, take the daily news trivia quiz, or link to an index of audio and video clips. The site has several other features that make it stand out. You can listen to ABCNews Radio live, take part in Sam Donaldson's live, Internet-only, video news program three times a week, or participate in an online bulletin board chat. You can access several interesting columns written by journalists who work for the network. Visitors also can get a preview of what news anchor Peter Jennings plans to cover in *World News Tonight*.

MSNBC
www.msnbc.com

E-mail: Click on Write Us.

Three media technologies are at work at MSNBC—broadcast, cable, and, of course, the Internet. From the first visit, you'll be prompted to personalize the news you can view. You will be asked to enter your ZIP code and the ticker symbols of three of your favorite stocks. If you take the time to do this, you can instantly see how your stocks fared during the day's trading, and you'll be able to see local headline news courtesy of the NBC affiliate in your area.

Another link on the home page allows you to further personalize your news experience. You'll also see a running list of headline news you can access with a click of the mouse.

Several things about this site make it stand out. For starters, MSNBC also has some nifty chat options. You can chat with NBC's John Hockenberry live, or you can watch *Feedback with John Gibson* and chat along with the show. Visitors also can link to the **Opinions** section of the site and send MSNBC their thoughts. (Careful now. MSNBC might just publish what you send.)

This site, which is part of the Microsoft Network, has wonderful multimedia features that allow visitors to see and hear the news. The video section is particularly nice, and the screen resolution seems to be a little bit better than what you'll find at other sites.

Once you're in the video section you can link to watch MSNBC cable news live or see video news clips from *The Today Show, NBC Nightly News,* and *Dateline NBC.* Indeed, one of the better features of this site is that it consolidates the news from several TV programs in one place.

Should you have any problems seeing or hearing any of the multimedia clips, click on **Cool Tools** and then **Multimedia Tools**. You'll be prompted to download some free software that will allow you to take advantage of the multimedia features at this site. These free tools have easy-to-follow installation instructions, and a series of screen prompts will guide you through the entire process.

Along the left side of the home page you'll see a list of categories for MSNBC's **News Menu**. You'll be prompted to download the **News Menu** if you click on some of the buttons in that section, such as technology. You'll also be

given the option to forgo the download and link directly to the section of information you're seeking. If you plan on visiting this site again, take a minute to download the **News Menu**. The entire process only takes a minute and it will ultimately save you time.

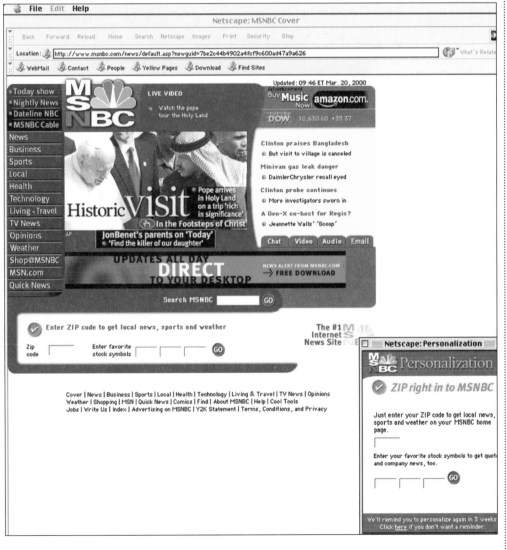

When you link to MSNBC's home page, you'll be prompted to enter your zip code and the ticker symbols of your favorite stocks. This will enable you to get headline news from the NBC affiliate nearest you and monitor your stocks online.

AccuWeather

www.accuweather.com

E-mail: ypaw@accuwx.com

Here are three good reasons why you might want to start getting your weather forecasts from the Web:

Reason #1: You have plans to go to the beach. You log on to AccuWeather and discover that it's supposed to rain all weekend at your destination. You opt to spend the weekend at a cabin in the mountains instead.

Reason #2: It's sunny where you are, but your flight home is routed through Denver. You log on and see that it's snowing like crazy there. You decide to call the airport first to see if your flight has been canceled or rerouted. You call home and let everybody know your flight has been delayed.

Reason #3: You're packing for that European vacation you've always dreamed about. You log on and check the 10-day forecast for Paris, France. It's unseasonably cool there this spring. You decide to add a few sweaters to your suitcase.

Indeed, Web weather forecasts have come to the aid of many a traveler or vacationer. Among the various weather-oriented sites on the Web, AccuWeather stands out as one of the best. Visitors can get information about the weather for 55,000 cities located worldwide at this Web site.

On the home page you'll be prompted to enter your zip code so you can view your local weather forecast. Along the left side of the page you'll find the main menu bar with links to the local, national, and international weather. You also can link to the hurricane center, view precipitation maps, check Doppler radar, and more.

A number of links warn visitors about severe weather, be it a thunderstorm or snowstorm. You also can sign up to get the latest AccuWeather forecast delivered to you via e-mail. This service is free.

However, some of the services provided at this site aren't free. A semicommercial site, AccuWeather provides additional services to its paying customers. For example, members get weather for virtually any spot on earth, 10-day forecasts, and access to current local, regional, and national NEXRAD Doppler radar. Only you can decide whether a subscription to this service is worth your money. Still, the freebies at this site make it well worth a visit.

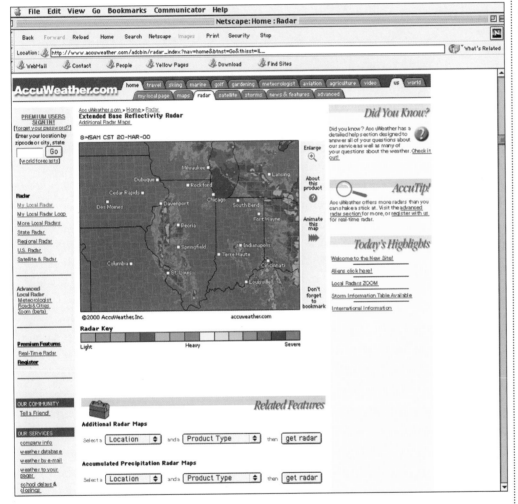

AccuWeather allows you to view Doppler radar for your area. You also can choose from a pull-down menu the type of Doppler radar you would like to use.

THE WEATHER CHANNEL

www.weather.com/homepage.html

E-mail: Click on Talk to Us.

You've seen the forecasts on cable TV, now check out The Weather Channel's Web site. Visitors will find weather-related news, educational material, a weather glossary, a storm encyclopedia, and seasonal features such as gardening conditions.

Golfers will definitely want to add this site to their Favorites folder. Before heading out to the links, log on and check out the current conditions using the **Golf Map**. You also can check out the weather conditions on the current pro tour, or set up a weekly planner to chart any weather conditions that might impact your game, such as turf conditions, wind speed, and wind chill.

Of particular interest to seniors is the **Health** link. Within this section you'll find national maps that show how weather conditions can affect your health. Those with arthritis might want to link to the **Aches & Pains** map. Other maps show what parts of the nation are being hit hard by the flu and what areas of the country are causing those with respiratory problems to experience some distress.

The weather maps, however, are really what attract visitors to this site. You can link to view local, regional, national, and international weather maps. Visitors also can click on a pull-down menu in this section to access current or severe weather information, get a two- or seven-day forecast, or see what Doppler radar and satellite images show. Other maps reveal earthquake activity.

In the **Travel** section, you'll find local flight information and airport delays. A number of travel maps and interstate maps also can be accessed. Clicking on the Interact link will take you to the message boards and chat rooms at this site. You can talk about severe weather events here, or sign up to get a free weather report delivered to you via e-mail.

Another feature of this site is it allows visitors to develop their own customized weather page. You can choose the news, forecast, and weather maps you would like to see displayed when you visit this site.

Not everything you'll find at The Weather Channel is serious, however. In fact, a few items are fun or just plain silly. For the curious, there are cameras that show the weather conditions in places like New York City, and there's a link that allows you to see the current weather conditions at the North Pole.

Is your arthritis bothering you? Log on to The Weather Channel's Web site and link to the **Aches & Pains** map. You also can link to maps that show where people are experiencing respiratory distress, have the flu, or are battling extreme temperatures.

Appendix

Sites for Seniors

AGE OF REASON
www.ageofreason.com
This is a fantastic jumping-off point for your searches on the Web. You won't find a lot of original content at this site, but you will find more than 5,000 links to Web sites of interest to seniors.

NATIONAL ASSOCIATION OF RETIRED FEDERAL EMPLOYEES (NARFE)
www.narfe.org
NARFE's Web site includes information about pending Congressional legislation that could affect retired federal employees' retirement and insurance benefits. You also can find the location of a local NARFE chapter in your area.

NATIONAL COUNCIL OF SENIOR CITIZENS
www.ncsinc.org
This organization works to protect the rights of older Americans. It tackles issues such as Medicare, Medicaid, Social Security, and affordable housing.

NATIONAL COUNCIL ON AGING (NCOA)
www.ncoa.org
Link to this site to find information about aging issues and advocacy programs supported by the NCOA. Visitors also can link to find a list of bills pending in Congress that are supported by the council.

RETIREMENT NET
www.retirenet.com
This site is a great resource for those considering retirement communities. Seniors can find information about active retirement communities, golf course communities, continuing care facilities, RV and resort communities, and more.

SENIOR CYBORGS
www.online96.com/seniors
This site's home page looks high-tech, but the information you'll find here is written in language that's easy to understand. The resources at this site are aimed at seniors, their loved ones, and their caregivers.

SENIOR LIVING ALTERNATIVES
www.senioralternatives.com

This site lists several living options for seniors, such as retirement communities, assisted living facilities, home health care, nursing homes, continuing care communities, and more. This online referral service is free, and you can sort the information you find by state.

Shopping

DRUGSTORE.COM
www.drugstore.com

This online store stocks a wide variety of over-the-counter medications. Visitors can get their prescriptions filled here through Rite Aid's online drugstore, or they can shop for vitamins and herbal remedies at General Nutrition Center (GNC).

HALLMARK
www.hallmark.com

This site has a great selection of online greeting cards. Visitors also can buy flowers and choose from more than 10,000 gift items, including videos of some Hallmark Hall of Fame movie collections.

H.O.T! COUPONS
www.hotcoupons.com

Forget about clipping coupons from the Sunday newspaper. Log on to H.O.T! Coupons. Enter your zip code, and H.O.T! Coupons will display a list of stores where you can use the site's online coupons.

INTERNET SHOPPING NETWORK
www.isn.com

This cybershop is more fun than the Home Shopping Network on your TV, which supplies many of the items visitors will find in the auction section. Jewelry lovers will appreciate the selection here as well.

MYSIMON
www.mysimon.com

MySimon takes the work out of comparison shopping. This site gathers, organizes, and presents up-to-date information about prices, shipping, and product warranties from thousands of online retailers so you can find the best deal on the Web. You also can use MySimon to search online auction sites and classified ads.

REALTOR.COM
www.realtor.com

This is a great site if you're looking for a retirement home in another state. You can search by city, neighborhood, or price, and find a realtor, a lender, and more.

SHOPPING.COM
www.shopping.com

Shoppers can find products and services from thousands of merchants, read product reviews and ratings, compare features and prices, and get a gift recommendation at this site, which is part of AltaVista.

Health

AMERICAN CANCER SOCIETY
www.cancer.org

The American Cancer Society site contains information about living with cancer, cancer research, prevention, treatment options, and more. Visitors also can link to get an overview of the different types of cancer.

ARTHRITIS FOUNDATION
www.arthritis.org

This nonprofit organization offers excellent information for individuals affected by arthritis. Seniors will find drug guides and good tips on how to manage their arthritis.

DISCOVERY HEALTH
www.discoveryhealth.com

If you like the Discovery Channel, you'll be equally pleased with their health Web site. Click on the Seniors' Health link to get the latest health and fitness news. You also can sign up to receive a free Seniors' Health e-mail newsletter.

HEALTHFINDER
www.healthfinder.org

Developed by the U.S. Department of Health and Human Services, Healthfinder helps visitors find online publications, clearinghouses, databases, Web sites, and support and self-help groups, as well as the government agencies and not-for-profit organizations that produce reliable information for the public.

HEART INFORMATION NETWORK
www.heartinfo.org

This educational Web site was founded by a heart patient and a physician. The information at this site, which ranges from nutrition guides to news articles, is comprehensive and well organized.

MENOPAUSE ONLINE
www.menopause-online.com

Visitors can find news and scientific studies, chat with others, and get up-to-date information about menopause. A board-certified gynecologist and menopause expert answers visitors' questions.

YOUR HEALTH DAILY
www.yourhealthdaily.com

The New York Times Syndicate runs Your Health Daily. This free service contains articles about a variety of different health topics from several leading daily newspapers.

Travel

AUTOPILOT
www.freetrip.com

This site is a godsend for the directionally impaired. AutoPilot allows you to create your own travel route, and then generates a list of motels and hotels, national parks, and other tourist sites you will pass along the way. You can also find out where ATMs and travel plazas are located en route.

FLIFO
www.flifo.com

Flifo specializes in discounted air fares. The best bargains here are for international travel. Visitors also can make rental car and hotel arrangements or check to see if an incoming flight is on time.

RV AMERICA
www.rvamerica.com

This site contains all the information needed to explore the RV lifestyle. Visitors can find online RV communities, resources for RV users, and names of RV dealers.

TRAVELNOW.COM
www.travelnow.com

This award-winning site is one of the best-kept secrets on the Web. If you're looking for an online travel reservation system that stresses simplicity and ease of use, this site is for you.

TRAVELOCITY
www.travelocity.com

This online travel reservation system lets visitors shop for air fares, rent cars, and book flights, hotel rooms, or their next cruise. Visitors also can find discount travel packages.

U.S. STATE DEPARTMENT TRAVEL WARNINGS
www.travel.state.gov/travel_warnings.html

Before you travel abroad, visit this site to see if the State Department has issued a warning advising Americans not to visit a particular country.

Financial Resources

BANK RATE MONITOR
www.bankrate.com

Bankrate.com provides consumers with financial data, research, and editorial information about non-investment financial products. The site is updated daily, and you can find the latest bank rates and news, and get information on credit card rates, auto loans, and more.

DOUGLAS GERLACH'S INVEST-O-RAMA
www.investorama.com

Douglas Gerlach has compiled a comprehensive set of links to financial resources on the Internet. If you need financial information, link here to browse Invest-o-Rama's directory of links. This site has several online guides that cover topics of interest to investors.

CHARLES SCHWAB
www.charlesschwab.com

Charles Schwab is one of the largest online brokers on the Web. Visitors can find investment tips, financial information, and more at this semi-commercial site.

FINANCENTER
www.financenter.com

This site contains interactive tools and calculators that can help you make personal finance decisions about home and auto loans, credit cards, insurance, and more.

MUTUAL FUND INVESTOR'S CENTER
www.mfea.com

Visit this site to get a good overall view of mutual funds. Visitors can search for a no-load mutual fund using 11 key investment criteria. Another feature allows investors to search for funds they can invest in for $50 or less.

QUICKEN
www.quicken.com

Financial software giant Quicken takes it to the Web with this site, which is filled with interactive tools that can help visitors do everything from tax preparation to retirement planning.

STOCK SMART
www.stocksmart.com

You can get a lot more than stock quotes at this site. Stock Smart has historical graphs, earnings reports, company news, and other information that can help investors do an in-depth investment analysis.

Hobbies

COOKING LIGHT
www.cookinglight.com

Those on a low fat or low calorie diet should check out this site. Visitors will find many of the same features that appear in *Cooking Light* magazine. This site can be searched by recipe, keyword, or ingredient.

GOLFWEB
www.golfweb.com

Created in association with CBS SportsLine, this site contains all kinds of information about what's happening on the PGA tour. Visitors also can find some articles covering events on the LPGA Tour.

Entertainment

ESPN SPORTS
www.espn.com

Part of the Go Network, ESPN provides well-rounded sports coverage of everything from the NFL to the NHL. The site has nice interactive features, such as video and audio links. Visitors can find scores, stats, and standings for their favorite teams.

FOX SPORTS
www.foxsports.com

You can find news stories, videos, message boards, and plenty of opportunities to meet and mingle with other sports fans at this site. You also can get the views and opinions of sports anchor John Madden.

MR. CRANKY
www.mrcranky.com

This movie reviewer's name says it all. Mr. Cranky's reviews and ratings, which range from "almost tolerable" to "as good as a poke in the eye with a sharp stick" are somewhat perverse, but on the money. Visitors can find a good guide to home-movie rentals at this site as well.

TV GUIDE ONLINE
www.tvguide.com

Can't find your *TV Guide*? Just log on to the company's Web site, and you can find cable, broadcast, and satellite listings, as well as feature stories, news, gossip, and information about your favorite soap operas.

News and Weather

BRITANNICA.COM
www.britannica.com

The Encyclopedia Britannica is online! You also can find numerous links to magazines, books, and other valuable news and reference materials at this site.

CNN Interactive
www.cnn.com

This well-rounded site offers some of the best online news videos on the Web. Visitors can customize their own news page, read headline news, or get information on topics ranging from finance to health.

New Choices
www.newchoices.com

Visitors can find information on health, travel, money, and even a few recipes at the New Choices Web site. This site also contains many articles that have appeared in this magazine, which is geared toward people aged 50 and older.

The New York Times
www.nytimes.com

You can find most of this daily newspaper's contents on its Web site. However, the content is revised throughout the day as breaking news is added. Visitors will find good financial and market news coverage.

Time.com
www.time.com

Time.com is a great source for daily news and information. This site contains a searchable archive, photo essays, online polls, and several other Web-based features that news junkies are sure to love.

The Washington Post
www.washingtonpost.com

There's nothing quite like reading a *Washington Post* writer's take on politics and politicians in and around our nation's capital. This well-designed site has an archive of articles visitors can search, and many good special sections.

USA Today
www.usatoday.com

Of the many newspapers that have established a Web site, *USA Today* is one of the best. This well-organized site is just as easy to scan as the newspaper.

Glossary

address book The place where people's names and e-mail addresses are stored on your computer. You can place commonly used addresses in this personalized list.

anti-virus program A program designed to remove and guard against computer viruses. Many anti-virus programs also repair files that have been damaged by a computer virus.

attachment A computer file electronically added to an e-mail message. Unlike a regular e-mail message, you usually must download, or transfer, an attachment to your computer's hard drive before you can open it and view it.

bandwidth The maximum amount of data that can be transferred per second between links in a network. Super-fast data networks form the backbone of the Internet.

Boolean logic Allows Internet users to refine their search by arranging keywords in a meaningful order and then searching for them as a phrase, rather than as individual words. This is done by using specific words or symbols—such as AND, OR, NOR, NOT, quotation marks, and plus and minus signs—to connect words and phrases in a search query. For example, putting the words "discount travel" in quotes searches for the words "discount" AND "travel" rather than "discount" OR "travel."

browser A software program that allows you to view information on the World Wide Web. Examples of browsers include Microsoft Internet Explorer, Netscape Navigator, and Opera.

cable modem Provides Internet connection speeds ranging from 400K to 4 megabits per second (Mbps). Examples of Internet cable providers include Time-Warner Road Runner and AT&T's Cable Network.

chat room Allows users to type and send messages that will be received instantly by other users located anywhere in the world.

computer network A group of computers that are physically linked together so they can share or exchange information.

computer virus Two of the most feared words in the English language. Computer viruses are software programs that are designed to destroy stored data or cause an undesired action to be performed by your computer.

digital subscriber line (DSL) An alternative to accessing the Internet via a standard modem. A DSL provides Internet access at speeds ranging from 144K to 1.7 Mbps.

domain name A suffix that signifies the type of site that is connected to the Internet. Common domain names include ".com," which stands for a company or corporation; ".gov," which stands for a government agency; ".mil," for military sites;

".edu," for educational institutions; ".net," which stands for a network; and ".org," for nonprofit organizations.

download The process by which an electronic file or software program is transferred from one computer to another. The Internet may act as the link between the two computers.

electronic commerce (e-commerce) Making purchases online or over the Internet. E-commerce is growing rapidly.

electronic mail (e-mail) Allows users to send and receive text, graphics, sounds, and videos to and from people all over the world. All e-mail addresses contain the user's name (or a fictional nickname), the @ symbol, and a domain name that indicates where the e-mail account resides, such as a company or government agency. In addition to a message, an e-mail may contain an attached file or graphic image.

full-text indexing A comprehensive type of Web indexing system in which every word on the Web page is put into a searchable database.

hard drive A computer's main internal storage device.

home page The entry page or main page of any Web site.

hyperlink A word, a group of words, an icon, or an image that will take you to a different document or another part of the same document when you click on it. Hyperlinks usually appear in a color that's different from the surrounding text.

hypertext markup language (HTML) The standard code used to create and format documents on the World Wide Web. HTML documents contain hyperlinks.

hypertext transfer protocol (http) The way Web pages are transferred over the Internet. All Web documents begin with http://, which lets your browser know the document is http-compatible.

icons A small graphic image that represents a specific file or program. To open the file or program, the user must click on the icon with the computer's mouse.

instant communication program A messaging program that allows users to send and receive messages instantly.

integrated services digital network (ISDN) A digital phone service capable of transferring data at speeds up to 128 kilobits per second.

Internet The computers, lines, routers, and other physical equipment that link millions of computers together.

Internet relay chat (IRC) *See* instant communication program.

Internet Service Provider (ISP) An organization that provides people with Internet access for a fee. ISPs may be national, regional, or local. Examples of national ISPs include AT&T WorldNet, Sprint Internet Passport, and MCI WorldCom Internet.

keyword A term that summarizes what you're trying to find on the World Wide Web.

keyword text indexing Puts words and phrases in a searchable database based on their location and frequency. If a word or phrase is only mentioned once or twice in the Web page, it may not be included in a keyword index.

kilobits per second (Kbps or K) A unit of measure that allows 1,000 bits of information to be transferred each second.

metasearch engine A Web search tool that sends one query to several major search sites and then displays the results. MetaCrawler is an example of a metasearch engine.

modem Short for modulator-demodulator, a modem is the device that lets a computer or set-top box "talk" to another computer through a standard phone line.

newsgroup An ongoing discussion on a particular topic, such as sports, TV shows, or politics. Newsgroups allow users to ask a question or respond to a question or message that is posted on an electronic bulletin board.

online service Contains "members-only" information that can't be found on the Web. Online services also provide their subscribers with a connection to the Web. Examples of online services include America Online (AOL), CompuServe, and Prodigy.

operating system The set of software programs that is necessary to control the basic operation of a computer. Windows 98 is an example of an operating system.

plug-and-play access Allows a computer to detect and configure a new piece of hardware automatically without making the user physically reconfigure certain hardware elements. Most new computers have plug-and-play access.

real time The ability to communicate with another Internet user or users without experiencing a delay.

satellite modem An alternative to accessing the Internet via a standard modem. Satellite modems will work anywhere there is open sky. Although a satellite modem can download information at speeds as fast as 400K, a regular modem and phone must be used to upload, or send, information across the Internet.

scroll bar Device that allows you to move up and down within a Web document.

search engine A program that allows users to locate specified information from a database. Search engines use keywords to examine Web documents. The search engine will then respond with a list of all the Web sites that match the query.

Secure Sockets Layer (SSL) The standard security protocol used on the Internet. SSL makes it extremely difficult for anyone to decode confidential information, such as credit-card numbers, that are sent across the Internet.

spam Net slang for unwanted or junk electronic mail.

surfing More Net slang that refers to the process of jumping from hyperlink to hyperlink with no particular information destination in mind.

toolbar A horizontal bar containing icons that give visual clues about a software program's capabilities. Icons within a Web browser's toolbar allow users to scroll back and forth between Web pages, print the material on the screen, and perform other functions.

Universal Resource Locator (URL) A standardized naming and addressing system used to pinpoint the location of documents and Web sites. A URL is often referred to as a Web address.

Web directory Sometimes referred to a subject tree, a Web directory divides information into broad topics. These topics are then divided into progressively smaller subtopics.

Web portal A site that includes links to other databases found on the Web. Portals may contain links to specialized news content, shopping sites, and other online services.

wildcard Prevents searchers from having to type multiple keywords that are similar. A wildcard is denoted by the * symbol. For example, the query "boat*" on AltaVista will return information on boats, boaters, boating, etc.

wireless modem An alternative to accessing the Internet via a standard modem. Wireless modems are capable of accessing the Internet at speeds that are 100 times faster than those provided by a cable modem or a digital subscriber line. Although this technology still is being perfected, wireless modems can provide users with an Internet connection from almost anywhere.

word stemming Allows users to search for grammatical variations of a search term. For example, the word "thought" will also return results for "think" and "thinking."

World Wide Web The graphical, user-friendly portion of the Internet that allows users to send information from one computer to another with ease.

Index

Using the CD-ROM

Playing Your CD-ROM

Windows®: Insert the CD-ROM into your CD-ROM drive. AutoRun automatically plays the software. You will see your screen go black before the CD-ROM begins to play. If AutoRun is disabled, double click on the Seniors icon. Then double click on the Start icon.

Macintosh®: Insert the CD-ROM into your CD-ROM drive. AutoRun automatically plays the software. You will see your screen go black before the CD-ROM begins to play. If AutoRun is disabled, double click on the Seniors icon. Then double click on the Start icon.

Windows® Start-Up Tips

These tips may help you start playing the CD-ROM on your PC if you are encountering difficulties. Also consult the Read Me file included on the CD-ROM or visit our Web site.
- Be sure your system meets the "Minimum System Requirements" listed on the cover.
- Check the CD for scratches or smudges. Clean gently with a soft cloth if needed.
- Set your display at 640×480 resolution and set colors to 256.
- Obtain the most current Windows® drivers from the manufacturer of your video card.
- Obtain the most current Windows® drivers from the manufacturer of your sound card.
- Close all Windows® applications before launching the CD-ROM.

Macintosh® Start-Up Tips

These tips may help you start playing the CD-ROM on your Macintosh® if you are encountering difficulties. Also consult the Read Me file included on the CD-ROM or visit our Web site.
- Be sure your system meets the "Minimum System Requirements" listed on the cover.
- Check the CD for scratches or smudges. Clean gently with a soft cloth if needed.
- Turn off your screen saver before running the CD-ROM.
- Close all open applications before launching the CD-ROM.

See Read Me file for helpful hints and other information.

Windows®: To open the Read Me file, double click on the My Computer icon. Right click on the CD-ROM icon and select Open. Double click on Readme.htm.

Macintosh®: To open the Read Me file, double click on the CD-ROM icon. Then double click on the Read Me file.

For support, visit our Web site at www.pubint.com.